LONDON'S BEST SHOPS & MARKETS

David Hampshire

Survival Books • Bath • England

First published 2016

Survival Books Limited
Office 169, 3 Edgar Buildings
George Street, Bath BA1 2FJ, United Kingdom
+44 (0)1225-462135, info@survivalbooks.net
www.survivalbooks.net and www.londons-secrets.com

British Library Cataloguing in Publication Data
A CIP record for this book is available
from the British Library.
ISBN: 978-1-909282-81-0

Printed in China

Acknowledgements

The author would like to thank all the many people who helped with research and provided information for this book. Special thanks are due to Ellie Broughton for her invaluable contributions to the Fashion and other chapters, Graeme & Louise Chesters and Di Bruce-Kidman; Robbi Atilgan for editing; Peter Read for editing and proof-reading; David Woodworth for final proof checking; John Marshall for DTP, photo selection and cover design; and the author's partner for the constant supply of tea, coffee, food and wine (and for continuing with the pretence that writing is a real job).

Last, but not least, a special thank you to the many photographers – the unsung heroes – whose beautiful images bring London's and markets shops to life.

The Author

David Hampshire's career has taken him around the world and he lived and worked in many countries before taking up writing full-time in the '80s. He's the author, co-author or editor of some 25 titles, including *London for Foodies, Gourmets & Gluttons, London's Cafés, Coffee Shops & Tearooms, London's Secret Places, London's Secrets: Museums & Galleries, London's Secrets: Parks & Gardens, London's Secrets: Peaceful Places* and *A Year in London*. David was born in Surrey but lived and worked in London for many years and still considers himself a Londoner. He now divides his time between London and Bath.

Readers' Guide

♦ **Contact details:** These include the address, telephone number and website (where applicable). You can enter the postcode to display a map of the location on Google and other map sites or enter the postcode into your satnav.

♦ **Opening hours:** These can change at short notice, therefore you should confirm times by telephone or check the website before travelling. Many stores are open seven days a week, although shopping hours on Sundays are restricted by law; many outlets also have late night shopping on one or two days a week. Note that some shops are only open 'by appointment'.

♦ **Public transport/parking:** Most shops featured are close to public transport (the nearest tube and/or railway station is listed), particularly in central London. Parking is often a problem in central London – although some stores have their own parking – and can be very expensive. Outside central London many stores provide free parking for customers.

♦ **Department stores:** You cannot beat London's department stores for one-stop shopping, which is why they have their own dedicated chapter (4) and also feature in the Fashion, Food & Drink, and Furniture & Homeware chapters.

♦ **Online shopping:** Almost all the shops featured have websites and offer online shopping, so it isn't necessary to travel to or live in London to enjoy the best of London shopping. Websites are also a good way to check and compare prices.

♦ **Prices:** As any shopper knows all too well, prices vary considerably depending on the retailer, the quality, and the manufacturer of goods. When comparing prices always ensure that you are comparing like with like, and beware of counterfeit goods, particularly when shopping in markets; if the price appears to be too good to be true, it probably is!

♦ **Fashion:** We have included a price guide for the fashion chapter (5), as the price range varies considerably, from cheap and cheerful to very expensive (for designer clothes).

♦ **Sales:** Many stores hold sales a few times a year, the traditional sales periods being January (New Year sales) and July (summer sales), although nowadays sales may be held throughout the year. It's the best time to restock your wardrobe and also to buy big ticket items, as prices are often slashed.

Contents

Introduction

The UK is a nation of diehard shoppers. Retail therapy is the country's favourite leisure activity – an all-consuming passion – and London is its beating heart. It's one of the world's most exciting shopping cities, packed with grand department stores, trend-setting boutiques, timeless

traditional traders, edgy concept stores, absorbing antiques centres, eccentric novelty shops, exclusive purveyors of luxury goods, mouth-watering food emporiums, bustling markets and much more. You'll find them all featured in the pages of *London's Best Shops & Markets*, including many hidden gems.

In the 18th century Napoleon allegedly dismissed England as 'a nation of shopkeepers' – and he wasn't wrong. Today there's an army of would-be entrepreneurs eager to follow in their ancestors' footsteps, despite the not inconsiderable financial risks, and make their fortune by ringing the tills. *London's Best Shops & Markets* is (with a few exceptions) a celebration of the city's independent shops, both traditional and avant-garde, many unique to the city and selling British (designed/manufactured) products; shops with lovely interiors, original goods, unique atmospheres and outstanding customer service. Independent retailers are the life and soul of any town – and London is no exception.

The city has its fair share of vast shopping centres, ubiquitous chain stores and supermarkets, yet small independent shops manage to survive (and even flourish) against the odds. Despite increasing competition, particularly from the internet, and the ever-present shadow of recession, London's independent shopping scene goes from strength to strength, and is constantly reinventing itself to meet the challenges of the 21st century.

Although it's possible to spend a king's ransom in London, particularly in Bond Street − one of the world's most expensive shopping streets − you don't need a bulging wallet to enjoy shopping. The city is one of the world's leading fashion centres, where great design is available to everyone whatever their budget – and browsing is free! Most stores hold at least two major sales a year (some seem to have permanent sales), traditionally in January and July, when you can snap up extraordinary bargains. For the shrewd shopper there's a wealth of discount stores, charity shops, markets, car-boot sales and auctions.

London boasts a huge number of lively markets, from the behemoths of Borough and Portobello to the bustling weekend honeypots of Brick Lane and Camden and the more sedate charms of Greenwich and Spitalfields. Markets are a rewarding hunting ground for savvy shoppers, selling everything from fresh fruit and vegetables to handicrafts and vintage clothes, artisan foods to household goods, secondhand books to collectibles. They're also great fun, particularly if you like haggling! Not much beats the thrill of finding a bargain and the city's flea markets are a great place to seek out hidden treasures.

Whether you want to revitalise your wardrobe or restock your larder, buy a new computer or an antique chair, track down a designer watch or a rare first edition − or find a gift for someone who's impossible to buy for − you're bound to find inspiration in *London's Best Shops & Markets*, which features some 300 of the capital's very best shopping destinations. We hope you will enjoy visiting them.

Happy Shopping!

David Hampshire
London, May 2016

Selfridges

Lots Road Auctions

1.
Antiques & Art

A city that fairly throbs with history and culture, London vies with New York to be the epicentre of the global antiques and art market. It offers a wealth of antiques shops, markets, auctions and fairs, and has a thriving art scene that encompasses a plethora of commercial art galleries, art fairs and some of the world's largest fine-art auctions

London's noble old auction houses, such as Christies and Sotheby's, are where national and international treasures change hands, be they old masters or modern art, jewellery or period furniture, rare porcelain or ethnic artefacts. But auctions can also throw up a bargain if you're a canny shopper, and nothing beats the thrill of a winning bid or a prize unearthed at one of the capital's art fairs or antiques markets.

London caters for all tastes and pockets, from billionaires seeking a Jackson Pollock for their Mayfair penthouse, to impoverished students looking for something to brighten up a drab bedsit. Whether you're a discerning collector or interior designer, an art buff or antiques enthusiast, or just seeking an interesting investment for your home − or maybe just a browser or people-watcher − you can indulge your every whim in London.

See also markets on page 199.

Alfies Antiques Market

The largest covered antiques market in the UK, Alfies occupies a huge Art Deco building on Church Street in Marylebone, formerly the home of Edwardian department store Jordan's, which closed in the '60s. After falling into disrepair, the store – which has a striking Egyptian-style Art Deco façade – was purchased in 1976 by property developer Bennie Gray (of Gray's Antiques Market – see page 24) and the market was named after his father. Since then it has expanded into a labyrinthine warren of adjoining buildings hosting around 100 specialist dealers in a chic bohemian atmosphere.

Most vendors specialise in 20th-century antiques and collectibles, including vintage fashion and accessories, modernist furniture, costume jewellery and 20th-century decorative arts. Frequented by serious collectors, interior designers, and theatre and television set designers, it's a great place to pick up Art Deco and '50s furniture, vintage clothes, and china from the likes of Clarice Cliff and Susie Cooper, along with trunks, lighting, paintings, silver, mirrors, glass, toys and much more. Shopping completed, relax in the rooftop café which boasts panoramic views over the city.

Alfies Antiques Market, 13-25 Church St, NW8 8DT (020-7723 6066; www.alfiesantiques.com; Marylebone tube/rail; Tue-Sat 10am-6pm, closed Sun).

Antiques & Art Fairs

London is one of the world's premier antiques and arts centres and host to some of its best antiques fairs. Whether you're a discerning collector, interior designer, an art or antiques enthusiast or simply looking for an interesting addition for your home, there's a wide range of events offering something for everyone. Featured below are some of the city's leading fairs which are supplemented by a host of smaller fairs throughout the capital; some run for a week while others are one-day events.

Launched by Will Ramsay in 2001, **The Affordable Art Fair** is held annually in Battersea (March) and Hampstead (June) – and around the world (see website) – showcasing over 150 unknown artists offering works costing from £100 to £5,000 (http://affordableartfair.com; Battersea Pk rail/Hampstead tube; 4 days; Mar/Jun/Oct).

The **Alexandra Palace Antiques & Collectors Fair** is London's largest antiques fair with over 200 stalls, held on several Sundays a year and organised by International Antiques & Collectors Fairs, organisers of the UK's largest antiques events. Better known as the Ally Pally Antiques Fair, it has been a firm favourite for decades and is a great place to pick up a bargain (www.iacf.co.uk/alexandra-palace; Wood Grn tube/bus; 1 day; Sun, see website for dates).

The BADA Antiques & Fine Art Fair – the showcase for members of the British Antique Dealers' Association – is held in Duke of York Square in Chelsea in March.

The week-long fair is one of the highlights of the London antiques scene and maintains an excellent reputation for quality and elegance (www.badafair.com; Sloane Sq tube; 7 days; March).

Established in 1950, **The Chelsea Antiques Fair** is London's longest-running antiques event, held over four days in March at Chelsea Old Town Hall. Now an annual event, the fair features around 40 dealers offering a huge variety of traditional art and antiques (www.penman-fairs.co.uk; Sloane Sq tube; 4 days; March).

> Penman Fairs (above) also organises the Chelsea Art Fair in April at Chelsea Old Town Hall, featuring many of the world's best and emerging artists.

Launched in 1985, **The Decorative Antiques & Textiles Fair** in Battersea was one of the first to combine antiques and interior design. It attracts over 100 exhibitors showcasing a range of fine and decorative antiques, 20th-century design, textiles and art. The fair is held three times a year – in spring, autumn and winter (see website for dates) – in beautiful Battersea Park (www.decorativefair.com; Battersea Pk rail; 6 days; see website for dates).

Held over five days in October in Regent's Park, **Frieze Masters** was established in 2003 and is one of the world's major art fairs. It brings together several thousand years of art in a unique, contemporary context, where visitors can view and buy art from over 130 of the world's best modern and historical dealers. Artworks include antiquities, Asian art, ethnographic art, illuminated manuscripts, medieval, modern and post-war art, old masters and 19th-century, photography, sculpture and *Wunderkammer* or cabinets of curiosities (http://friezemasters.com; Mornington Cres tube; 4 days; October).

Since its inception in 2009, the **LAPADA Art & Antiques Fair** in Berkeley Square has grown to become one of London's foremost international showcases for art and antiques, as well as one of the most prestigious events on the London social

LAPADA is the acronym for the Association of Art & Antiques Dealers, the largest organisation of professional art and antiques dealers in the UK.

calendar. It attracts around 100 exhibitors from across the art, antiques, design and decorative arts spectrum, including dealers in jewellery, furniture, carpets, tapestries, antiquities, clocks, ceramics, silver and fine art (www.lapadalondon.com; Bond St/Green Pk tube; 6 days; September).

Established in 2010, **Masterpiece** is London's newest international antiques and art fair and one of the capital's most glamorous. Held at the iconic Royal Hospital Chelsea, the fair showcases museum-quality works with impeccable provenance from over 150 leading dealers and galleries worldwide. Exhibits span 4,000 years of art history, from antiquity to the present day (www.masterpiecefair.com; Sloane Sq tube; 7 days; June/July).

The week-long **Olympia International Art & Antiques Fair** is the UK's largest art and antiques fair, taking place twice a year in summer (June) and winter (November) at the Kensington Olympia Exhibition Centre. It's one of the most prestigious antiques fairs in the UK, hosting 100-150 of the world's finest specialist dealers offering a wide choice of high quality, vetted art and antiques (www.olympia-art-antiques.com and www.olympia-antiques.com; Kensington Olympia tube/rail; 7 days; June & November).

The Other Art Fair is the UK's leading showcase for the best emerging artistic talent. Whether you're a first-time buyer or a seasoned collector, the fair  offers something for everyone, featuring some 130 contemporary artists working in a range of styles and mediums with artworks starting from as little at £50 (www.theotherartfair.com; Holborn tube; 4 days; April).

Bayswater Road Artists

On Sundays throughout the year, come rain or shine, Bayswater Road is transformed into the world's largest regular open-air art show. For more than 50 years artists have been displaying their original works (no prints) along the railings of Kensington Gardens; these include some who have exhibited at the Royal Academy, a smattering of international names and unknowns who could be the Picasso, Pollock or Hockney of tomorrow.

Some 150 artists turn up each Sunday to display thousands of paintings, sculptures, enamels and collages, with subjects ranging from contemporary abstracts and traditional landscapes to the tiniest miniature flower paintings. All exhibits are for sale at studio prices – you may even snap up a bargain!

Bayswater Road Artists, Bayswater Rd, W2 2UD (www.bayswater-road-artists.co.uk; Lancaster Gate/Queensway tube; Sun 10am-6pm).

Bermondsey Market

Until relatively recently, Bermondsey Market was notorious as a venue where thieves could legally sell their swag with impunity; a royal licence (*marché ouvert*) which meant that goods sold there from sunset to sunrise didn't require provenance was repealed only in 1995.

It's now home to Bermondsey Square Antiques Market: part car boot sale, part chic Parisian flea market, good for bric-a-brac, collectibles and antiques, and all manner of bizarre ephemera, although you need to arrive early to get the best pickings (many dealers shop here). An added bonus is the excellent range of local cafés and restaurants, offering some of the best breakfasts in town.

Bermondsey Antiques Market, Bermondsey Sq, SE1 3UN (http://bermondseysquare.net/ bermondsey-antiques-market; Borough tube; Fri 6am-2pm).

Bonhams

Founded in 1793, Bonhams is one of the world's oldest and largest auctioneers of fine art and antiques. In 2000, the family-owned company merged with specialist auctioneer Brooks; this (with further acquisitions) helped forge the dynamic

21st-century auction house we see today, with offices in prime locations around the globe. Its flagship London saleroom – on prestigious New Bond Street in Mayfair – was redesigned in 2011-13 to create striking new salerooms and offices.

Holding some 400 sales annually across its 60 departments, Bonhams offers a wealth of art and furniture sales and also stages frequent specialist sales in areas such as scientific instruments, classic and vintage motor cars, ceramics, coins, rock 'n' roll and sporting memorabilia. Pre-sale viewings are open to the public, so you can browse even if you can't afford to buy.

With specialists in every major area of art and collectibles, the depth of collective knowledge of Bonhams' auctioneers has enabled the company to become world leaders in many key areas of the UK art market, often achieving record prices. You can book a free valuation with one of these experts, and the auction house also hosts valuation events (see website).

Bonhams, 101 New Bond St, W1S 1SR (020-7447 7447; www.bonhams.com; Bond St tube; Mon-Fri 9am-5.30pm, closed Sat-Sun).

Camden Passage Antiques Market

Visiting Camden Passage – an 18th-century cobblestoned alley running along the backs of houses on Islington's Upper Street – is like stepping back in time. It's home to a row of elegant Georgian antiques shops, pubs, cafés and

restaurants, and on Wednesdays and Saturdays hosts a multitude of stalls selling an eclectic mix of antiques and collectibles: vintage clothes, handbags, jewellery, silver, porcelain and assorted bric-a-brac.

Whether you're a dealer, designer, collector or just a curious browser, you'll find Camden Passage Antiques Market (not to be confused with Camden Market in Camden Town – see page 205) intriguing. Most of the traders are specialists who know their onions, so just chatting with them can be an education as well as a lot of fun, but you need to arrive early and haggle hard to get a bargain.

The camaraderie of the traders has enabled the Passage to survive where other antiques markets have failed. Standards have remained consistently high and the wide range of quality goods has ensured its enduring success as a centre of excellence. The main antiques market is held twice weekly, although there are smaller markets on some other days and the larger shops are also open daily or by appointment.

Camden Passage Antiques Market, Camden Passage, N1 8EA (www.camdenpassageislington. co.uk; Angel tube; Wed & Sat 9am-6pm).

Christie's

The world's oldest and foremost fine art auctioneer, Christie's was founded in 1766 by James Christie, since when it has grown into a worldwide powerhouse with over 50 offices in some 32 countries and salerooms in cities including London, New York, Paris, Geneva, Milan, Amsterdam, Dubai, Zürich, Hong Kong, Shanghai and Mumbai. Now owned by Groupe Artémis, the holding company of French billionaire François-Henri Pinault, its global headquarters are in St James's (King Street) in London, where the auction house has been sited since 1823.

Today, Christie's conducts some 450 auctions worldwide annually covering all areas of fine and decorative arts, jewellery, photography, collectibles, wine and more. It has two London salerooms, at its HQ in St James's and in South Kensington. Open seven days a week, Christie's South

Kensington is the busiest saleroom in the UK, holding over 100 sales annually with a total of over 30,000 lots. Sales dedicated to home furnishings (interiors) are held monthly alongside those of single-owner collections and specialist collectors' sales throughout the year.

Christie's offers a no-obligation valuation service by appointment (Mon-Fri 9am-5pm) at its South Kensington offices.

Christie's, 8 King St, SW1Y 6QT (020-7839 9060; www.christies.com; Green Pk tube; Mon-Fri 9.30am-4.30pm) and 85 Old Brompton Rd, SW7 3LD (020-7930 6074; S Kensington tube; Mon 9am-7.30pm, Tue-Fri 9am-5pm, Sat-Sun 11am-5pm).

Commercial Art Galleries

As one of the world's major art centres, London has a wealth of commercial galleries – a selection of which are featured below – that hold frequent exhibitions of old masters, 19th- and 20th-century British and continental art, and leading British and international contemporary artists. For a comprehensive list of London's commercial galleries, see www.london-galleries.co.uk.

Catto Gallery: Established in 1986, the Catto Gallery in Hampstead has grown to become one of the most prestigious fine-art galleries in London, specialising in the best of contemporary art across all mediums. It was founded by Gillian Catto and taken over in 2009 by two employees, Iain Barratt and Imogen Green, who between them have over 20 years' experience in the business. New exhibitions are held around every three weeks, showing unique works by pre-eminent artists from around the globe.

Catto Gallery, 100 Heath St, NW3 1DP (020-7435 6660; www.cattogallery.co.uk; Hampstead tube; Mon-Sat 10am-6pm, Sun 12.30-6pm).

> There are two further branches of the Gagosian Gallery in London, at 17-19 Davies St, W1K 3DE and 20 Grosvenor Hill, W1K 3QD.

Gagosian Gallery: Owned and directed by Larry Gagosian, one of the world's best international art dealers, the cavernous Gagosian Gallery is part of an international chain which includes three galleries in London and others in New York, Paris, Rome, Athens, Geneva and Hong Kong. Located in King's Cross, the gallery attracts collectors, art buffs and students alike, and hosts regular shows by important contemporary artists such as Richard Prince, Hiroshi Sugimoto and Rachel Whiteread.

Gagosian Gallery, 6-24 Britannia St, WC1X 9JD (020-7841 9960; www.gagosian.com; Kings Cross/St Pancras tube; Tue-Sat 10am-6pm, closed Sun-Mon).

Hauser & Wirth: Founded in Zürich in 1992 by Iwan Wirth, his wife Manuela and mother-in-law Ursula Hauser, H&W is a European super-gallery devoted to contemporary and modern art. It launched in London in 2003 (on Piccadilly) and since 2010 has been in Savile Row where it has two vast galleries with separate entrances. The gallery has a reputation for supporting radical installation artists, in addition to a regular exhibition programme featuring a glittering roster of critically-acclaimed artists such as Paul McCarthy, Diana Thater and Martin Creed. It also looks after the estates of Eva Hesse, Lee Lozano and Jason Rhoades.

Hauser & Wirth, 23 Savile Row, W1S 2ET (020-7287 2300; www.hauserwirth.com; Oxford Circus tube; Tue-Sat 10am-6pm, closed Sun-Mon).

the conventional contemporary art market, and is considered to be the international market leader in what is dubbed urban art, although many of its artists defy categorisation.

Lazarides Gallery, 11 Rathbone Pl, W1T 1HR (020-7636 5443; www.lazinc.com; Tottenham Court Rd tube; Wed-Sat 11am-7pm, closed Sun-Mon, open by appointment Tue).

Lazarides Gallery: A constant force in championing the careers of influential artists, Lazarides has grown into an internationally-acclaimed gallery. Set in the heart of Fitzrovia, the gallery exhibits many of the most significant artists who thrive outside

Lisson Gallery: Founded in 1967 by Nicholas Logsdail and Fiona Hildyard, Lisson is one of a handful of pioneering international galleries to champion the careers of a generation of artists associated

with Minimalism and Conceptual art.
For nearly half a century, the gallery has
supported generations of artists – including
important names such as Anish Kapoor, Sol
LeWitt, Richard Deacon and Ai Weiwei –
each with a radical and distinctive approach
to art.

**Lisson Gallery, 27 Bell St, NW1 5BY and 52 Bell
St, NW1 5BU (020-7724 2739; www.lissongallery.
com; Edgware Rd tube; Mon-Fri 10am-6pm, Sat
11am-5pm, closed Sun).**

Matt's gallery has an unusual inspiration. It
was named after director Robin Klassnik's
dog, Matt E Mulsion.

Matt's Gallery: A contemporary art space
established in Hackney by Robin Klassnik in
1979, Matt's moved to its current premises
in 1993. It's a not-for-profit gallery, funded
by the Arts Council and other major trusts
and foundations, which exists to support
artists with the time and space to take risks,
test their limits, and develop their ideas
and techniques. Artists are generally at
the young or emerging end of their career
spectrum and exhibitions vary widely in
scope, but are invariably interesting.

**Matt's Gallery, 42-44 Copperfield Rd, E3 4RR
(020-8983 1771; www.mattsgallery.org; Mile End
tube; Wed-Sun noon-6pm, closed Mon-Tue).**

Parasol Unit:
The Parasol Unit
Foundation for
Contemporary
Art (to give it
its full name)
was founded
in 2004 and is
a registered
educational
charity. Housed
in a classic old
warehouse
building, the gallery's impressive minimalist
design is by Italian architect Claudio
Silvestrin and has 5,000ft^2 of exhibition
space. Internationally recognised for its
forward-thinking and challenging exhibition
programme, Parasol has introduced a host
of international artists to London's public and
been instrumental in launching the careers
of artists such as Michaël Borremans, Yang
Fudong and Charles Avery.

**Parasol Unit, 14 Wharf Rd, N1 7RW (020-7490
7373; www.parasol-unit.org; Angel/Old St tube;
Tue-Sat 10am-6pm, Sun noon-5pm, closed Mon).**

Philip Mould & Co: Unlike many of the
other galleries featured here, which deal
mostly or exclusively in contemporary works
of art, Philip Mould & Co (director Philip

Philip Mould

Mould OBE is better known as the co-host of the BBC TV show *Fake or Fortune*, which attempts to authenticate unattributed works of art) is a leading specialist dealer in British art and old masters. Recently relocated to splendid new premises on Pall Mall, the gallery offers a large selection of fine paintings for sale, from Tudor and Jacobean panel pictures to 18th-century landscapes, as well as works by old masters such as Titian and Van Dyck and antique portrait miniatures.

Philip Mould & Co, 18-19 Pall Mall, SW1Y 5LU (020-7499 6818; www.philipmould.com; Piccadilly Circus tube; Mon-Fri 9.30am-6pm, closed Sat-Sun).

Victoria Miro Gallery: One of the grandes dames of the Britart scene, Victoria Miro opened her first gallery on Cork Street in Mayfair in 1985, earning widespread acclaim for showcasing the work of established and emerging international artists and nurturing the

careers of young British artists. In 2000, the gallery relocated to an 8,000ft² converted furniture factory on Wharf Road, in the shabby no-man's land between Islington and Hoxton. Expanded in 2006 with the opening of Victoria Miro 14 − a 9,000ft² exhibition and viewing space − it's one of the largest and most dramatic commercial art spaces in London.

Victoria Miro Gallery, 16 Wharf Rd, N1 7RW (020-7336 8109; www.victoria-miro.com; Angel/Old St tube; Tue-Sat 10am-6pm, closed Sun-Mon).

The Victoria Miro Gallery is almost unique in London for having its own garden, a beautiful landscaped area overlooking a restored stretch of Regent's Canal. It has been used to great effect for installations by artists such as Japan's Yayoi Kusama (below).

warehouse, an auditorium and a bookshop. It has been a strong influence on the British contemporary art scene over the last decade or so, with its list of artists comprising a who's who of British and international cutting-edge art: from Tracey Emin, Damien Hirst and Jake & Dinos Chapman to sculptor Antony Gormley and photographers Gregory Crewdson and (Jopling's ex-wife) Sam Taylor-Wood.

White Cube Gallery, 144-152 Bermondsey St, SE1 3TQ (020-7930 5373; http://whitecube.com; London Br tube/rail; Tue-Sat 10am-6pm, Sun noon-6pm, closed Mon).

White Cube: Opened in 2011, White Cube in Bermondsey was art dealer Jay Jopling's third London gallery. At a massive 58,000ft², it is not only the largest art gallery within the White Cube empire but also the largest commercial gallery in Europe – and is achingly cool. The former '70s warehouse contains three major exhibition spaces, private viewing rooms, office space, a

The **Fine Art Society**

The Fine Art Society is one of the world's oldest art dealerships. They've been doing business on New Bond Street since 1876, so bring a wealth of experience and history to their trade. Specialising in British art and design from the 19th to the 21st centuries – particularly the Victorian period – they offer a huge choice of paintings, prints and antique furnishings and decorative items, including textiles.

As you might expect, prices tend to be high, but so is the quality. They also have a branch on Dundas Street in Edinburgh.

The Fine Art Society, 148 New Bond St, W1S 2JT (020-7629 5116; http://faslondon.com; Bond St tube; Mon-Fri 10am-6pm, closed Sat-Sun).

Furniture Cave

Spread over three floors, the Furniture Cave – recently renamed the Furniture and Arts Building (FAB), but the old name sticks – is a group of over 20 individual dealers trading under the same roof. The building extends to 30,000ft^2 and is crammed with antique and vintage furniture, reproduction furniture and contemporary designer pieces, plus assorted silver, jewellery, paintings, ceramics and glass. It's a treasure trove for discerning private buyers, dealers and interior designers, although you need to know your stuff and bargain hard to ensure you don't pay over the odds. There's also a restoration department and a café.

The Furniture Cave, 533 King's Rd, SW10 0TZ (020-7352 6116; www.furnitureandartsbuilding. co.uk and www.furniturecave.co.uk; Fulham Broadway tube; Mon-Sat 10am-6pm, Sun 11am-5pm).

Grays Antiques Market

Based in an attractive (Grade II listed) Victorian terracotta building, Grays is an antiques centre opened in 1977 by antiques dealer and entrepreneur Bennie Gray (also owner of Alfies Antiques Market – see page 10). It's home to around 100 dealers and even has its own uniformed doorman. The dealers specialise in most periods and styles from Georgian to Edwardian, Art Nouveau to Art Deco; the front of the market tends to house the more expensive pieces, including high-end antique gems with four-figure price tags.

An interesting historical feature is the water channel in the basement (stocked with goldfish), which is part of the famous 'lost' River Tyburn.

Grays Antiques Market, 58 Davies St & 1-7 Davies Mews, W1K 5AB (020-7629 7034; www. graysantiques.com; Bond St tube; Mon-Fri 10am-6pm, Sat 11am-5pm, closed Sun).

Hampstead Antique & Craft Emporium

A popular destination for collectors and enthusiasts since 1967, Hampstead Antique & Craft Emporium – tucked just behind Heath Street – is a hidden gem with over 25 independent dealers. It's packed with everything from antique and vintage furniture and collectibles to contemporary design and craft items.

Dealers specialise in jewellery, Art Deco, mid-century, ethnic and modern styles, including period and contemporary silverware, watches, clocks, oriental art, ceramics, textiles, glassware, furniture, paintings, kitchenalia, vintage fashion and accessories, and much more. There's also a Lebanese café (Tania's).

Hampstead Antique & Craft Emporium, 12 Heath St, NW3 6TE (020-7794 3297; www. hampsteadantiqueemporium.com; Hampstead tube; Tue-Fri 10.30am-5.30pm, Sat 10am-6pm, Sun 11am-5.30pm, closed Mon).

Kensington Church Street

Kensington Church Street, running from Notting Hill Gate to Kensington High Street, is one of London's most interesting shopping streets, particularly for antiques. The street (and its surrounds) is home to over 60 of the city's top antiques dealers – many of whom exhibit at the world's most prestigious antiques fairs – offering fine art and antiques from the Tang dynasty to the Art Deco movement. Visiting KCS is like visiting an antiques fair that's open all year round, with exhibits including Japanese and Chinese ceramics and other oriental works of art; European porcelain and pottery; English and continental furniture; silver and 20th-century decorative arts; Indian and Islamic antiquities; and much more.

Kensington Church St, W8 (www.antiques-london.com; High St Kensington/Notting Hill Gate tube).

London Silver Vaults

Situated on Chancery Lane in the City, the London Silver Vaults were established in 1953 and house the world's largest collection of fine antique silver. Originally built as a safe deposit in 1876, it's an underground maze of around 30 silver dealers, each with an individual shop or vault. Their wares range from small items – cufflinks, spoons, card holders and rings – to much grander pieces such as bowls, pots and urns.

They include contemporary silver as well as antique gems from master silversmiths such as Paul de Lamerie (1688-1751) and Paul Storr (1771-1844), along with pieces from famous designers like Christopher Dresser (1834-1904) and Archibald Knox (1864-1933).

London Silver Vaults, Chancery Ln, WC2A 1QS (020-7242 3844; http://silvervaultslondon.com; Chancery Ln tube; Mon-Fri 9am-5.30pm, Sat 9am-1pm, closed Sun).

Lots Road Auctions

Recently made more famous by Channel 4's fly-on-the-wall documentary *The Auction House*, Lots Road Auctions in Chelsea was established in 1979 by Roger Ross (a joint founder of The Furniture Cave – see page 23). It provides an ever-changing eclectic assortment of both contemporary and antique items, ranging from Persian rugs to Matisse etchings, Titchmarsh & Goodwin hand-crafted furniture to Art Deco gems. In addition to the weekly Sunday auctions – held at noon (modern items) and 3pm (antiques and decorative) – there are regular specialist sales in fields including fine antiques, continental furniture, lighting and mirrors, silver, carpets, tribal and Asian art and artefacts, and Russian art.

Lots Road Auctions, 71-73 Lots Rd, SW10 0RN (020-7376 6800; www.lotsroad.com; Fulham Broadway tube/Imperial Wharf rail; Mon-Tue, Thu, Sun 9am-6pm, Wed 9am-8pm, Fri 9am-5pm, Sat 10am-5pm, check website for viewing and valuation times).

Northcote Road Antiques Market

Founded in 1986, Northcote Road Antiques Market in Battersea is one of London's best-value antiques centres, home to some 30 freelance dealers. The huge variety of stock includes everything from classic 19th and early 20th-century pieces to Art Deco and '50s classics, French painted, country pine, vintage and retro.

There are specialist dealers in many fields including ceramics and glass objets d'art; vintage costumes and jewellery; original prints and watercolours; antique silver and clocks; Georgian furniture and chandeliers; retro kitchen utensils and art pottery. You'd be hard pressed to find a more diverse collection anywhere else in the country.

Northcote Road Antiques Market, 155A Northcote Rd, SW11 6QB (020-7228 6850; www. northcoteroadantiques.co.uk; Clapham Junc rail/Clapham S tube; Mon-Sat 10am-5.30pm, Sun noon-5pm).

The Old Cinema

A former Edwardian picture palace relaunched for retail in 1979, the Old Cinema antiques centre on Chiswick High Road styles itself as an 'antique, vintage, and retro department store'. Boasting 10,000ft^2 of showrooms, this family business

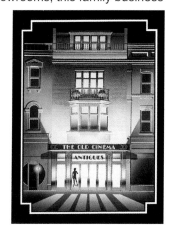

is home to a collective of antiques dealers, decorators, designers, artisans and jewellers, offering a vast eclectic range of stock. A favourite with collectors, dealers and designers, the ever-changing inventory makes the Old Cinema a great shopping destination, offering everything from kitsch Americana to period antiques, Arts & Crafts to Art Deco, *Mad Men*-style rosewood to hardcore industrial. It also specialises in painted furniture and upcycled items.

The Old Cinema, 160 Chiswick High Rd, W4 1PR (020-8995 4166; www.theoldcinema.co.uk; Turnham Grn tube; Mon-Sat 10am-6pm, Sun noon-5pm).

Old Spitalfields Market

One of London's finest surviving Victorian market halls, located in East London just outside the City, Old Spitalfields Market is a popular daily market trading in fashion, footwear, bric-a-brac, vintage, antiques, art, produce (selected Fridays) and general goods. Mondays to Wednesdays and Sundays are general market days, while on Saturdays there are themed markets (see website). The best days for antiques and art are Thursdays and Fridays; on Thursdays traders offer an eclectic range of vintage collectibles and antiques, while Fridays are a mecca for vintage fashion fans and art lovers. There's also a record fair on the first and third Fridays and second Saturday of the month. Affordable and great fun.

Old Spitalfields Market, 109 Commercial St, E1 6BG (020-7247 8556; www.oldspitalfieldsmarket. com; Liverpool St tube/rail; Thu-Fri 10am-5pm).

Phillips

Founded in London in 1796 by Harry Phillips – early clients included Marie Antoinette, Beau Brummel and Napoleon Bonaparte – Phillips has grown to be one of the world's principal auction houses, specialising in 20th- and 21st-century contemporary art. It was acquired in 2008 by luxury retail company the Mercury Group, and in 2014 moved to a state-of-the-art European headquarters and salesrooms – with 31,000ft^2 of space – in exclusive Berkeley Square.

Based in New York and London, with offices throughout the world, Phillips conducts sales in a select number of categories: contemporary art, photography, editions, design, jewellery and watches. Its core art services also includes special exhibitions, private sales, advising private estates and corporate clients, museum services and consulting.

Phillips is synonymous with contemporary art and culture and claims to be 'the most dynamic and forward-looking of the international auction houses' through its focus on the defining aesthetic movements of the last 50 years. There's always something interesting on show at the pre-auction viewings – it recently held an auction of David Beckham photographs – and is well worth a visit, even if most prices are in the lottery-winners' league.

Phillips, 30 Berkeley Sq, W1J 6EX (020-7318 4010; www.phillips.com; Bond St/Green Pk tube; Mon-Sat 10am-6pm, Sun noon-6pm).

Photographers' Gallery

The Photographers' Gallery in Soho – the largest public gallery in London dedicated solely to photography – offers inspiration for everyone, from phone snappers to professionals. There's a packed

schedule of exhibitions, talks, events, workshops and courses, as well as a working *camera obscura*, study room and print sales gallery, where you can learn about, discover and buy photography, whatever your level of interest or budget. The gallery holds a wide range of works, including exclusive limited edition prints, and offers expert advice to help buyers invest wisely and enjoyably in photography. At street level there's a bookshop and a café/bar.

Photographers' Gallery, 16-18 Ramillies St, W1F 7LW (020-7087 9300; www. thephotographersgallery.org.uk; Oxford Circus tube; Mon-Sat 10am-6pm and till 8pm Thu during exhibitions, Sun 11am-6pm).

Piccadilly Market

Held in the courtyard of St James's Church – one of Christopher Wren's finest churches and reputed to be his favourite – Piccadilly Market is a charming and vibrant market on one of London's busiest streets. Established in 1984, it runs from Monday to Saturday each week, selling a diverse range of food, gifts, arts, crafts, antiques and collectibles. On Monday there's a food market, followed on Tuesday by an antiques and collectibles market, while from Wednesday to Saturdays it's the turn of the arts and crafts market. While you're here, take some time to visit the church and its garden; there's also an excellent café.

Piccadilly Market, St James's Church, 197 Piccadilly, W1J 9LL (020-7734 4511; http:// piccadilly-market.co.uk; Piccadilly Circus tube; Tue-Sat 10am-6pm).

Portobello Market

One of London's longest established shopping streets, Portobello Road gets its exotic name from the Panamanian town of Portobelo, captured by the British from the Spanish in 1739 during the intriguingly named War of Jenkins' Ear. It's now a west London landmark and home to Portobello Market, which celebrated its 150th anniversary in 2015. This is actually several markets rolled into one, including Portobello Green Market and Golborne Road Market (see page 217), although the Saturday antiques market is the star turn.

Said to be the world's largest antiques market, it takes place every Saturday when over 1,000 dealers set up stalls along the stretch of road (roughly) between Chepstow Villas and Elgin Crescent. The market starts slowly at around 5.30am and most dealers are in place by 8.30am. It's best to get there before10am as an hour later the market is heaving. Some traders shut up shop after lunch but many stay until late afternoon.

The market is a great day out even if you aren't into antiques, with numerous excellent local cafés and restaurants to sustain you. But be prepared to haggle over the price and be wary of fakes (and pickpockets).

Portobello Market, Portobello Rd (Chepstow Villas to Elgin Cres), W11 (www.portobelloroad. co.uk, www.portobellomarket.org/antiques.htm and http://shopportobello.co.uk; Notting Hill Gate/Ladbroke Grove tube; Sat 5.30am-5pm).

Sotheby's

Like its old rival Christie's, Sotheby's is a byword for fine art and a London institution. It operates from some 90 locations in 40 countries and today has its worldwide HQ in New York, although the company was founded by a London book dealer, Samuel Baker (one half of Baker

and Leigh) in 1744. The current business dates back to 1804, when two partners of the original business (Leigh and Sotheby) left to set up their own book dealership. Now the world's fourth-oldest auction house, it moved from the Strand to Mayfair's New Bond Street in 1917.

Sotheby's auctions offer an extraordinary diversity of objects and works of art – it's the largest art business in the world – from impressionist, modern and contemporary art to old masters, 19th-century European to Islamic art, decorative porcelain and silver to French and English furniture. Sotheby's auctions cover more then 50 categories, including jewellery, fine wine, furniture, watches, motor vehicles and real estate. It often makes the headlines as in February 2015, when an auction featuring impressionist and modern works by Monet, Matisse and Picasso broke the record for the highest sales total ever reached at a London auction: £186.44m.

Rare among auction houses, Sotheby's has an excellent café serving breakfast, lunch and afternoon tea.

Sotheby's, 34-35 New Bond St, W1S 2RT (020-7293-5000; www.sothebys.com; Oxford Circus tube; Mon-Fri 9am-5pm, Sat-Sun viewing only).

Daunt Books, Marylebone

2.
Books

As the capital of the English-speaking and publishing world, London has always had a thriving bookshop scene. However, since the demise of the Net Book Agreement in the '90s – which fixed the retail price of books – the rise of discounters and online sellers has resulted in the closure of hundreds of UK bookshops. Nevertheless, the death of the independent bookshop has been greatly exaggerated, in the capital at least.

If anything, the increased competition has forced the city's independent booksellers to up their game. Those that have survived – and thrived – have done so by exploiting literary niches, providing characterful service from well-read staff, and offering a café-style shopping experience that you simply can't get on the web. Independent bookshops have filled the gaps left by high-street chains, stocking thoughtful and idiosyncratic choices rather than ubiquitous best-sellers; they include everything from general bookshops to those specialising in areas such as travel, children's, art, secondhand, foreign-language, academic and even cookery.

London's bookshops are a joy to browse, where you'll make discoveries that you never would on Amazon. Long may they flourish!

Books for Cooks

A bookshop dedicated to food, cooking and eating, Books for Cooks is a mecca for cooks, chefs, foodies, gourmets and gluttons. The shelves are crammed with over 8,000 tasty titles, while a comfy sofa is provided for browsers seeking inspiration. Once discovered you'll wonder how you ever survived without Books for Cooks.

It was founded by Heidi Lascelles in 1983, when a bookshop selling nothing but cookery books must have seemed a decidedly risky venture in Britain's culinary wasteland at that time. But Heidi quickly gained an enviable reputation and a large international clientele for her willingness to track down books and dispatch them to buyers in far-flung corners of the globe.

Today, Books for Cooks is much more than a bookshop – it's an internationally renowned, epicurean epicentre for food

lovers everywhere. It's also one of the best-smelling shops in London, thanks to the staff's reputation for 'cooking the books'; they put recipes to the test in their kitchen at the back of the shop and sell the results in their charming inexpensive café. And if reading and tasting isn't enough, cookery classes are held in the demonstration kitchen upstairs.

Books for Cooks, 4 Blenheim Cres, W11 1NN (020-7221 1992; www.booksforcooks.com; Ladbroke Grove tube; Tue-Sat 10am-6pm, closed Sun-Mon).

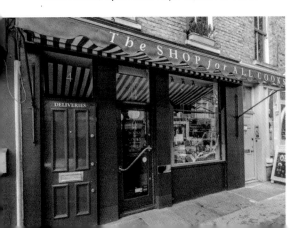

Daunt Books

Founded in 1990 by James Daunt, now the MD of Waterstones (see page 53), the Daunt flagship store on Marylebone High Street is housed in a beautiful Edwardian bookshop dating from 1912 and believed to be the first custom-built bookshop in the world. The back room is particularly impressive, with its original oak mezzanine gallery, graceful skylights and stained-glass window. Entering Daunts is like rewinding to a calmer, more graceful era, when people had time to browse and customer service wasn't just a cliché – staff are knowledgeable, while the books are beautifully displayed.

Though not strictly a travel bookshop, this lovely shop is seen first and foremost as a travel specialist thanks to its elegant three-level back room, home to row upon row of guide books, maps, language reference books, history, politics, travelogues and related fiction organised by country. Daunt is also good for literary fiction, biography, gardening and much more.

Daunt Books has only been trading for 25 years – a relatively short time in the book

world – but now has six shops and an enviable reputation as one of London's most treasured independent booksellers. If that's not tempting enough, there's also a cosy café providing the perfect opportunity to savour your tomes over a warming cup of something.

Daunt Books, 83 Marylebone High St, W1U 4QW (020-7224 2295; www.dauntbooks.co.uk; Baker St tube; Mon-Sat 9am-7.30pm, Sun 11am-6pm).

Dulwich Books

This West Dulwich bookshop celebrated its 30th anniversary in 2013 and has been lauded as one of the country's best. Dulwich Books was voted London's Best Independent Bookshop in 2012 and 2013, and the UK & Ireland Best Independent Bookshop 2014 by trade magazine *The Bookseller*. It's now owned by one of its most loyal customers, Susie Nicklin, who bought the shop in 2015.

Dulwich Books stocks over 8,500 titles – children's and adults', fiction and non-fiction – and specialises in providing personal recommendations. It's very much a community bookshop, engaging closely with authors, customers, schools and colleges. One of the secrets of the shop's success is its comprehensive programme of readings and signings – attracting a plethora of celebrity authors – including readings for young children on Thursday and Saturday mornings. It stocks

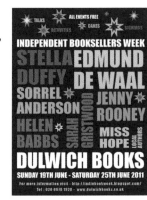

greetings cards, gift stationery/wrap, magazines, literary journals, notebooks, diaries and calendars, plus a range of educational games for children. And it offers eBooks via its website and in store.

You can sign up to Dulwich Books' email newsletter on their excellent website but do pay a visit. Bookworms are spoilt for choice in SE21, as there's another award-winning bookshop in Dulwich Village: see Village Books (page 52).

Dulwich Books, 6 Croxted Rd, West Dulwich, SE21 8SW (020-8670 1920; http://dulwichbooks. co.uk; West Dulwich rail; Mon-Sat 9.30am-5.30pm, Sun 11am-4pm).

The European Bookshop

Owned by the ESB group of Cheltenham, the European Bookshop – incorporating the Young Europeans Bookstore and Italian Bookshop – has been supplying expatriates, language students and others with foreign-language publications for over 40 years, and is widely recognised as one of the best foreign-language bookshops in the world.

ESB is the UK's leading specialist distributor, wholesaler and retailer of books in European languages other than English. Everything in their catalogue is normally kept in stock, alongside the latest continental literature, important language titles from UK publishers and an excellent children's section.

The European Bookshop, 123 Gloucester Rd, SW7 4TE (020-7734 5259; www. europeanbookshop.com; Gloucester Rd tube; Mon-Fri 9.30am-6.30pm, Sat 10am-6.30pm, closed Sun).

The Folio Society

Founded by Charles Ede in 1947, The Folio Society publishes beautifully crafted, imaginative editions of the world's great works of fiction and non-fiction, and sells them in its Holborn bookshop. The books selected for publication are timeless and offer a rich literary experience for readers of all ages. They are designed to be cherished, handled with

pleasure, read and reread, and handed down to the next generation.

A Folio book is a unique object, one in which typography, illustration, paper, and printing and binding techniques all play a part in creating a harmonious whole. And as you'd expect, the bookshop is an Aladdin's cave for booklovers and devotees of great literature.

The Folio Society, 44 Eagle St, WC1R 4FS (020-7400 4200; www.foliosociety.com; Holborn tube; Mon-Fri 10am-5pm, closed Sat-Sun).

Fosters' Bookshop

Established in 1968, this family-run bookshop occupies the oldest shop on Chiswick High Road, dating from the late 18th century and Grade II listed. It's now managed by (second generation) Stephen Foster, whose claims to fame include sourcing rare books for the film industry, including many James Bond movies. Fosters specialise in antiquarian books, fine bindings, illustrated children's books and first editions, as well as general stock leaning towards literature and the arts.

The antithesis of book chains like Waterstones or (heaven forbid!) Amazon, Fosters is a booklover's dream with classic books overflowing from floor-to-ceiling shelves and piled high on every available surface, and an intoxicating aroma of old books.

It offers something for all tastes and budgets, starting from as little at £2 for

books on the outside tables and bookcases to hundreds of pounds for antique gems such as Victorian editions of Dickens, not forgetting original framed watercolour paintings, maps and lovely greetings cards. If you cannot make it to the shop, you can browse the database of over 7,000 hard to find, out of print, used and rare books on their online shop (www.95bellstreet.com).

Fosters' Bookshop, 183 Chiswick High Rd, W4 2DR (020-8995 2768; www.fostersbookshop. co.uk and www.95bellstreet.com; Turnham Grn tube; Tue-Sat 10.30am-5.30pm, closed Sun-Mon).

Foyles

Founded in 1903 – and still run by the Foyle family – world-famous bookseller Foyles opened its new flagship store in 2014 at 107 Charing Cross Road, a few doors along from the iconic rabbit warren of a store it had occupied for over a century.

Foyles is one of Europe's largest bookshops with 37,000ft^2 of retail space spread over four floors, four miles of shelves and over 200,000 titles. An impressive full-height central atrium and large windows fill the space with natural light – a world away from the dusty nooks and crannies of the old building – while the layout allows for easy navigation and the serendipitous discovery of new books.

Aside from works of general fiction, Foyles also holds a huge stock of non-fiction titles on every subject under the sun. Following its takeover of foreign-language specialist bookseller Grant & Cutler in 2011, it's also one of the UK's largest foreign-language retailers with titles covering every living language from Afrikaans to Zulu – and even some dead ones too.

Alongside books, there's a wide range of gifts and stationery, magazines, printed music, classical music CDs, classic and world DVDs, as well as Ray's Jazz (a specialist music store), a café and an auditorium. Foyles also has a number of smaller stores across the city.

Foyles, 107 Charing Cross Rd, WC2H 0DT (020-7437 5660; www.foyles.co.uk; Tottenham Court Rd tube; Mon-Sat 9.30am-9pm, Sun noon-6pm).

Hatchards

Hatchards is London's oldest bookshop and the second-oldest in the UK (after the Cambridge University bookshop). It was founded by John Hatchard in 1797 on Piccadilly, from where it still trades today, although a modern version opened in 2014 in St Pancras station. The original Hatchards is the city's most aristocratic of bookshops, situated opposite the Royal Academy. Customers have included most of Britain's greatest political, royal, social and literary figures – from Queen Charlotte (it boasts three Royal Warrants) to Disraeli, Gladstone to Wellington, Kipling to Lord Byron.

fireplaces and five floors of small inter-linked rooms clustered around a central winding staircase. It stocks more than 100,000 titles, stacked from floor to ceiling, covering almost every topic with the genres of travel, fiction, history and biography particularly well represented. There's even a wall of antiquarian books dedicated to Winston Churchill.

Hatchards is a heady mix of old-world character and personal service, and a favourite with both writers and readers. As such, it has a stellar reputation for attracting famous authors for signings/readings, from JK Rowling to David Attenborough, Sebastian Faulks to Michael Palin.

Hatchards, 187 Piccadilly, W1J 9LE (020-7439 9921; www.hatchards.co.uk; Piccadilly Circus tube; Mon-Sat 9.30am-7pm, Sun noon-6pm).

Although it's now owned by Waterstones, Hatchards retains the spirit of bygone days, with an interior reminiscent of a rambling old house; dark wood panelling, original

Heywood Hill

Occupying two floors of a Georgian townhouse in the heart of Mayfair opposite Shepherd's Market, Heywood Hill has been supplying the worthy citizens of London with reading material since 1936 – it's noteworthy for having employed Nancy Mitford, eldest of the famous Mitford sisters, as the manager during World War Two – and today is owned by Peregrine 'Stoker' Cavendish, 12th Duke of Devonshire,

whose family have long been supporters of the shop. Selling new and rare antiquarian books, as well as producing catalogues on numerous themes, it specialises in literature, history, architecture, biography and travel, and also has a children's department stocked with the best new and classic titles.

Today, Heywood Hill is a literary landmark in its own right; generations of writers, readers and collectors from across the English-speaking world have flocked to this little shop, which describes itself as 'an outpost of civilisation and a place where good writing and beautiful books really matter'.

The staff are brilliant: dedicated bibliophiles who delight in matching books and customers and go out of their way to learn their clients' reading tastes in order to offer a tailored literary service. They delight is helping customers discover something unexpected that's perfectly suited to them.

Heywood Hill, 10 Curzon St, W1J 5HH (020-7629 0647; www.heywoodhill.com; Green Pk tube; Mon-Fri 9.30am-6pm, Sat 9.30am-5pm, closed Sun).

John Sandoe Books

John Sandoe opened his celebrated bookshop in 1957 and it's since become a Chelsea institution. This lovely shop occupies three floors of a beautiful 18th-century building off the King's Road and, although moving with the times, remains essentially the same: an independent literary bookshop catering to book-loving regulars. Space is limited, yet they still manage to shoehorn in some 25,000 books, packed from floor to ceiling, stacked up the stairs and piled on tables. Every surface displays treasured tomes.

John Sandoe was 'a prince among booksellers' and his legacy lives on today. He was bought out by a group of his employees in 1989 – and the new owners are full of love for their subject, which is reflected in the wealth of books on offer, the artful displays, and the service which is prompt and courteous, erudite and enthusiastic.

This isn't a shop in which to pick up the latest blockbuster bestseller, but rather an invaluable resource for professionals, a treasure trove for discerning readers and a delight for browsers. Not surprisingly, JS has legions of fans who praise everything about it: the amazing stock, the clever use of space, the obliging staff and the beautiful catalogues. John Sandoe makes buying books the pleasurable, exciting experience it should be.

John Sandoe Books, 10 Blacklands Ter, SW3 2SR (020-7589 9473; www.johnsandoe.com; Sloane Sq tube; Mon-Sat 9.30am-6.30pm, Sun 11am-5pm).

London Review Bookshop

The London Review Bookshop in Bloomsbury is owned by the celebrated literary journal, the *London Review of Books* (www.lrb.co.uk), and opened in 2003 a stone's throw from the British Museum. It's one of London's most distinctive independent bookshops: an attractive space with a lovely ambience, offering an eclectic, well-chosen range of books that can be browsed in peace and quiet.

The LRB stocks the widest array of books imaginable (general interest and scholarly tomes – no blockbusters here) within a space that's easy to navigate. The passionate and highly knowledgeable staff care about their stock and their customers. The bookshop also functions as a forum for literary presentations and intellectual exchanges through a series of readings, discussions and lectures that are always

engaging and interesting. You can sign up to its newsletter on its excellent website.

However, the LRB is much more than 'just' a bookshop and also houses one of the city's most popular cafés: the London Review Cake Shop. It's a haven for booklovers, coffee connoisseurs and cake-a-holics, serving such sweet editions as rose and pistachio cake and rich chocolate and Guinness cake. It's a great example of how to turn a bookshop into a social hang out – a modern-day literary coffee house.

London Review Bookshop, 14 Bury Pl, WC1A 2JL (020-7269 9030; www.londonreviewbookshop. co.uk; Holborn tube; Mon-Sat 10am-6.30pm, Sun noon-6pm; cake shop closed Sun).

Lutyens & Rubenstein

L utyens & Rubinstein is a beloved bijou bookshop opposite the Kitchen & Pantry in Notting Hill. Founded in 2009 by literary agents Sarah Lutyens and Felicity Rubinstein, it's the perfect spot for a bit of browsing for discerning readers – a companionable and idiosyncratic experience

for people who love books. The eye-catching window displays, tasteful black and white decor, artful book displays, cute little mezzanine level and bookish ceiling decorations lend this lovely shop a sophisticated air. And browsing is actively encouraged, with places to sit and read without any pressure to buy, aided and abetted by the tiny coffee shop downstairs.

The stock (4,000 tomes – quality not quantity!) comprises a cleverly curated but expansive range of fiction, non-fiction, poetry, graphic novels, children's classics and coffee-table tomes, with the emphasis on writing excellence and narrative. The core stock was put together by canvassing hundreds of readers – writers, publishing

contacts, friends (both adults and children) – about which books they would most like to find in a bookshop. Thus every book stocked has its place because somebody loves it and has recommended it. See the website for a range of book subscriptions and bespoke services.

Lutyens & Rubinstein, 21 Kensington Park Rd, W11 2EU (020-7229 1010; www.lutyensrubinstein. co.uk/bookshop-homepage; Ladbroke Grove tube; Mon, Sat 10am-6pm, Tue-Fri 10am-6.30pm, Sun 11am-5pm).

Maggs Bros. Ltd

Established in 1853, Maggs is one of the world's largest antiquarian booksellers and the holy grail for collectors of rare books. Appropriately housed in a fine 18th-century townhouse in the heart of Mayfair, it was founded by Uriah Maggs (a Dickensian name, if ever there was one), who at the age of 25 left his home town of Midsomer Norton in Somerset to set up business in London.

Maggs sells books and manuscripts of the highest quality and acts as an advisor and bookseller to many of the world's finest collections, both private and institutional, in addition to stocking more affordable books at a wide range of prices.

Maggs Bros. Ltd, 46 Curzon St, W1J 7UH (020-7493 7160; www.maggs.com; Green Pk tube; Mon-Fri 9.30am-5pm, closed Sat-Sun).

Newham Bookshop

Like all good bookshops, the Newham Bookshop is a pillar of the community. Established in 1978, it was originally financed by local people who each donated £5 and is run as a non-profit company with a board of directors but no owner. Founded as part of the service of the fledgling Newham Parents' Centre to provide a source of books, education and play materials, it's a true community bookshop, catering for students, teachers, parents and the whole local populace.

In these tough times when bookshops and libraries everywhere are closing their doors, Newham Bookshop isn't just surviving, it's thriving. It's East London's largest independent bookshop and the perfect model for communities everywhere.

Newham Bookshop, 745-7 Barking Rd, E13 9ER (020-8552 9993; www.newhambooks.co.uk; Upton Pk tube; Tue-Fri 9am-5pm, Sat 10am-5pm, closed Sun-Mon).

Pages of Hackney

A bijou bookshop on 'murder mile' on the Lower Clapton Road – the shop was once the local post office until the postmaster was shot dead in a robbery – Pages of Hackney stocks an eclectic selection of contemporary and classic fiction, travel, children's, politics, environment, art, cookery and more. There's also an excellent secondhand section in the basement, full of Penguin classics and children's books.

Opened in 2008 by Eleanor Lowenhall (who lives above the shop), Pages quickly became a thriving community and cultural hub. It won the Mayor of Hackney's Business Awards' Best New Business and was shortlisted for the *Bookseller* Independent Bookseller of the Year in 2010 and 2011.

It holds regular author events, readings and art exhibitions in its basement gallery, and hosts a book group on the last Monday of each month; it has a mailing list for information about events (contact info@ pagesofhackney.co.uk). In addition, Pages offers a book-ordering service (you can collect most books the next day) as well as searching for out-of-print books. All in all, it's a classic community bookshop.

Pages of Hackney, 70 Lower Clapton Rd, E5 0RN (020-8525 1452; http://pagesofhackney.co.uk; Hackney Downs rail; Mon-Fri 11am-7pm, Sat 10am-6pm, Sun noon-6pm).

Persephone Books

F ounded in 1998 by Nicola Beauman, Persephone is an independent publisher based in Bloomsbury which reprints books by female writers (mostly from the mid-20th century) that have been largely neglected for the past 50 years. Their collection of some 115 books (and rising) includes novels, short stories, diaries, memoirs and cookery books, each with an elegant dove-grey cover and a 'fabric' endpaper with matching bookmark. The beautiful books are complemented by the lovely bookshop, situated in an early 18th-century building near Great Ormond St Hospital and a haven of tranquillity.

Persephone Books, 59 Lamb's Conduit St, WC1N 3NB (020-7242 9292; www.persephonebooks. co.uk; Russell Sq tube; Mon-Fri 10am-6pm, Sat noon-5pm, closed Sun).

Primrose Hill Books

T his wonderful little bookshop, owned and run by Jessica Graham and Marek Laskowski, has been a local landmark in Primrose Hill for over 25 years. Inside there's a well-chosen selection of titles, both hardback and paperback, including bestsellers and reference books, travel guides and a good mystery section. There's also a fine collection of children's books, including all the favourites plus a selection of lesser-known titles discovered over the years. The shop also specialises in rare and out-of-print books and has an assortment of secondhand books.

Primrose Hill Books, 134 Regent's Park Rd, NW1 8XL (020-7586 2022; www.primrosehillbooks. com; Chalk Farm tube; Mon-Fri 9.30am-6pm, Sat 10am-6pm, Sun 11am-6pm).

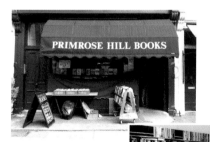

The Society Club

A classy cocktail of bookshop, gallery, café and bar, the Society Club is one of London's most interesting and original 'offerings' and one with a deserved cult following. Owners Robert and Babette Pereno set out to offer 'the best of all possible things' and have succeeded admirably. Elegant and cosy, it's like a delightfully eccentric Bohemian sitting room, where you're sure of a warm welcome.

The Society Club stocks an eclectic range of books, from rare signed first editions to the latest bestsellers, and there are some interesting specialist sections dedicated to 'vintage erotica', 'Soho literature', '20th-century modern 1st editions' and 'pulp fiction'.

The shop-cum-club also serves as a photograph gallery and hosts monthly shows, where all the exhibits are for sale. Other events include book launches, author talks and readings, poetry readings, music and much more – see the website (upcoming events) for information. If you really like the place, you can become a member, and there's a second branch in Shoreditch. So drop in for a browse, admire the photos, pet the dogs, sip a cocktail – it's a bookshop with a magical twist!

The Society Club, 12 Ingestre Pl (corner of Silver Pl & Ingestre Pl), W1F 0JF (020-7437 1433; www. thesocietyclub.com; Piccadilly Circus tube; Mon-Sat noon-6pm, members 6-11pm, closed Sun).

Southbank Centre Book Market

One of London's best-kept secrets, the Southbank Centre Book Market on Queen's Walk (under Waterloo Bridge) is the city's only secondhand and antiquarian book market. Setting up their stalls daily, come rain or shine, these booksellers are London's answer to the *Bouquinistes* who ply their trade along the Seine in Paris: they are experts dealing in rare, old, hardback editions of the classics,

manuscripts, poetry, art books, maps, photographs and prints, plus a wealth of secondhand paperbacks.

It's a great place to search for a rare first edition, but you don't have to be an avid collector to enjoy this book haven – it's for anyone who doesn't want (or cannot afford) to pay bookshop prices or is looking for an out-of-print title. If you're seeking a particular book you're likely to find it here for a fraction of its original price and usually in good condition. Not as cheap as a car boot or charity shop, but a lovely spot to browse and maybe pick up a pre-loved bargain.

The book market is a great place to while away a lunch hour or a lazy Sunday morning, and when you've had your fill of books you can pop into the Southbank Centre for a drink or meal.

Southbank Book Market, beneath Waterloo Bridge/Queen's Walk, SE1 (www. southbankcentre.co.uk/visitor-info/shop-eat-drink/shops/southbank-centre-book-market; Waterloo tube; daily, early to 7pm).

Stanfords

Stanfords in Covent Garden is London's foremost specialist map and travel book store, and the world's largest travel bookshop. Established by Edward Stanford in the 1850s as a map publisher, the imposing Long Acre shop (in Flemish renaissance style) opened in 1901 selling maps, travel books, globes and travel-related goods.

In its early days Stanfords was the first port of call for explorers, empire-builders and travelling salesmen, supplying maps of the world when a third of it was coloured pink. Nowadays it serves the likes of Bill Bryson, Ranulph Fiennes and Michael Palin, plus a legion of intrepid backpackers, trekkers, weekenders and tourers.

It's a wonderful browsable bookstore, set over three storeys, that remains the best place in London to pick up guides, maps, travelogues, coffee table tomes and travel-related objects of all kinds – if Stanfords doesn't have it then it probably hasn't been published. They also stock atlases and antique maps and guides, plus a range of equipment such as medical kits, binoculars and torches. And you can plan your latest expedition over a coffee and cake in the lively Antipodean-style Sacred Café on the ground floor.

The shop also stages regular signings, lectures and other events; sign up to the email newsletter to receive information.

Stanfords, 12-14 Long Acre, WC2E 9LP (020-7836 1321; www.stanfords.co.uk; Covent Gdn tube; Mon-Sat 9am-8pm, Sun noon-6pm).

Tales on Moon Lane

A previous winner of the Walker Independent Children's Bookshop of the Year at the *Bookseller* Industry Awards, Tales on Moon Lane is an enchanting children's bookshop in Herne Hill, south London, owned by Tamara Macfarlane. Specialising in books for children of all ages, from toddlers to teenagers, the shop offers all the classics such as the Narnia series and Beatrix Potter, the contemporary giants JK Rowling and Philip Pullman alongside the best up-and-coming children's authors.

The shop is a magnet for children (and parents), with weekly storytelling sessions combining singing, stories and music, phonics' workshops for toddlers and a dedicated kids' book group. At half term TML runs teachers' reading groups and frequently hosts book fairs and author and illustrator visits to schools, as well as staging the Moon Lane Children's Literature Festival. It also provides a schools' reading advisory service from experienced teachers and knowledgeable staff.

If you cannot visit the shop but would like some book recommendations, check out their website (and teen blog) which has an Essential Reading Guide featuring reviews of the best new and classic titles.

Tales on Moon Lane, 25 Half Moon Ln, SE24 9JU (020-7274 5759; http://talesonmoonlane.co.uk and http://teensonmoonlane.co.uk; Herne Hill rail; Mon-Fri 9am-5.45pm, Sat 9am-6pm, Sun 10.30am-4.30pm).

Village Books

Located in the heart of lovely Dulwich Village, Village Books is one of two superb, award-winning independent bookshops that cement Dulwich's reputation as a draw for booklovers (the other is Dulwich Books, see page 36). First launched in the '30s, it's been run since 1996 by Hazel Broadfoot and Julian Toland, who honed their skills at Waterstones. Spread over two floors, it stocks all the latest bestsellers together with a wide selection of fiction, biography, history, travel, cookery and much more.

An integral part of the community, Village Books is a centre of cultural excellence and has an army of loyal customers who praise it to the heavens for its enthusiastic, friendly and knowledgeable staff, efficient ordering service, helpful reading suggestions and literary events. It will introduce you to a

treasure trove of books and writers, not only on paper but in person: the shop has a busy programme of author events and welcomes a stream of novelists, historians, actors, famous cooks and children's writers (you can sign up to their mailing list online to keep up to date with future events).

And if you're a dog lover as well as a booklover, your four-legged friend will also be made at home and welcomed with doggy treats!

Village Books, 1D Calton Ave, SE21 7DE (020-8693 2808; http://village-books.co.uk; N Dulwich rail; Mon-Sat 9am-5.30pm, Sun 11am-5pm).

Waterstones, Piccadilly

With some 275 book stores, Waterstones is the UK's last remaining major chain of general bookshops which has somehow managed to survive in an era when many bookshops are closing. It was founded by Tim Waterstone in 1982, and since 2011 has been owned by Russian billionaire Alexander Mamut and managed by James Daunt, owner of Daunt Books (see page 35). The company also owns Hatchards (see page 40), located just a few doors away.

The chain's flagship store on Piccadilly – set in a beautiful '30s Art Deco building, formerly Simpsons' department store – is Europe's largest bookshop, with six floors and more than eight miles of bookshelves, containing over 200,000 different titles.

The store offers something for everyone, whatever your taste, including comprehensive fiction, travel, history and art sections, plus a children's department modelled on a (Piccadilly) circus theme with a range of activities and events. In addition, there's a selection of beautiful first-edition books, a comprehensive events programme (from visits by luminaries such as Hillary Clinton to readings by members of the Royal Academy), as well as a complimentary gift-wrapping service and worldwide shipping. There's a café on the mezzanine floor and a bar/restaurant on the 5th floor offering great views.

Waterstones, 203/206 Piccadilly, W1J 9HD (020-7851 2400; www.waterstones.com/bookshops/piccadilly; Piccadilly Circus tube; Mon-Sat 9am-10pm, Sun noon-6.30pm).

Apple Store, Covent Garden

3.
Computers, Electronics & Music

London has long been a magnet for music fans, movie buffs and technophiles. The city is home to many brands' vast flagship stores, from Apple to HMV, along with numerous celebrated independent shops catering for collectors and enthusiasts. It's famous for its wealth of music stores – selling everything from musical instruments to avant-garde CDs – electronics outlets (hi-fi equipment, computers, home cinema, etc.) and camera shops. Some London streets have traditionally specialised in certain wares, such as Denmark Street for sheet music and guitars and Tottenham Court Road (Oxford Street end) for home electronics and photography, which remains so today.

This chapter covers the whole spectrum of technology and entertainment on offer in the capital, from hi-fi and home cinema to camera equipment (new and secondhand), vintage vinyl to rare CDs, and state-of-the-art laptops to electronic gadgetry. Featured stores include international giants such as Bang & Olufsen and Yamaha, but also niche stores like Graham's Hi-Fi and Honest Jon's record shop. You'll be spoiled for choice.

The Apple Store, Covent Garden

If you're an Apple fan, a techie or just curious as to what all the fuss is about, then a visit to Apple's award-winning Covent Garden store to check out the company's iconic products is both an education and a treat. When it opened in 2010 it was the company's 300th store and the largest Apple store in the world, usurping the Regent Street store as London's flagship.

It occupies a striking historic building, brought bang up to date with clever use of glass (stairway, elevator shaft and stairways), steel and wood. Centred round an airy atrium, the spacious store covers

three floors and has separate rooms (each with exposed brickwork, oak tables and stone floors) dedicated to different iconic products: iMacs, MacBooks, iPads, iPhones, iPods and Apple Watches.

Services include a special 'Start Up' room, where you can get free assistance to set up your new Apple product the moment you've bought it, a community room for advanced workshops and a Genius Bar where Apple techies are on hand to answer your Apple-related questions and solve software/hardware problems. Whether you're an Apple addict or just love beautiful gadgets, this is the place to get your fix.

Apple Store, No. 1-7 The Piazza, WC2E 8HB (020-7447 1400; www.apple.com/uk/retail/coventgarden; Covent Gdn tube; Mon-Sat 10am-8pm, Sun noon-6pm).

Ask

Ask has been a fixture on Tottenham Court Road – London's hub for technology and electronics – for over 30 years. Established in 1983, this family-owned store is one of the UK's leading independent retailers of consumer electronics. With 10,000ft² of retail space spread over four floors, it's also one of the largest, stocking the latest and best

technology from the world's leading brands, including computers, cameras and camcorders, televisions and radios, audio and hi-fi, plus hard-to-find accessories. Prices are competitive and after-sales service is excellent. There's also a 'click and collect' service that allows you to place an order online and pick up your purchase from the store.

Ask, 248 Tottenham Court Rd, W1T 7QZ (020-7637 0353; www.askdirect.co.uk; Tottenham Court Rd tube; Mon-Sat 10am-7pm, closed Sun).

Bang & Olufsen

One of the most iconic names in hi-fi and television, Danish company Bang & Olufsen (founded 1925) are renowned for the beautiful design, innovation and quality of their products. Their London flagship store in Hanover Square contains a concept showroom which 'delivers a sensory experience through sound and design' with a dedicated revolving speaker wall and demonstration zones, a uniquely furnished home cinema room, and a play area where you can listen to the latest range of headphones and portable/digital sound systems. The combination of technological excellence, aesthetic appeal and audio-visual quality is hard to beat.

Bang & Olufsen, 21 Hanover Sq, W1S 1JW (020-7495 8898; http://stores.bang-olufsen.com/great-britain/bang-olufsen-hanover-square; Oxford Circus tube; Mon-Sat 10am-6pm, closed Sun).

CeX

Formed in London in 1992, CeX (short for Complete Entertainment Exchange) was created by a group of like-minded people who were seeking somewhere they could obtain secondhand technology and entertainment products at knockdown prices. Today CeX remains an independent company, but has grown into a worldwide chain with over 400 stores in the UK, Australia, India, Ireland, Italy, the Netherlands, Mexico, Poland, Portugal, Spain and the USA.

CeX buy, sell and exchange a range of technology and entertainment products, including mobile phones, video games, DVDs and Blu-ray movies, computers, digital electronics, TVs and music CDs. All purchases come with a 12-month warranty, whether bought from a store or online.

CeX, 70 Tottenham Court Rd, W1T 2HB (0845-345 1664; https://uk.webuy.com; Goodge St tube; Mon-Sat 10am-7pm, Sun 10.30am-4.30pm).

Currys PC World

One of the UK's largest retail chains of mass-market electrical and computer superstores, Currys PC World is owned by Dixons Carphone. Dixons bought Currys in 1984 and PC World in 1993, and since 2009 many stores have been dual-branded as Currys PC World, including the one featured here on Tottenham Court Road − a one-stop shop for computer, television, hi-fi, camera and home appliance products. If you need another reason to visit, in 2015 Google opened its first-ever branded shop in this store selling the company's range of Android phones and tablets, Chromebook laptops and Chromecast TV services.

Currys PC World, 145-149 Tottenham Court Rd, W1T 7NE (0344-561 0000; www.currys.co.uk/ www.pcworld.co.uk; Tottenham Court Rd tube; Mon-Fri 9am-8pm, Sat 9am-7pm, Sun noon-6pm).

Denmark Street

Running from Charing Cross Road to St Giles in London's West End, Denmark Street has been associated with British popular music since the '50s, first through its publishers and later its recording studios – it was once the UK's 'Tin Pan Alley' – and music shops. A blue plaque was unveiled in 2014 commemorating the street's importance to popular music.

Now being redeveloped, Denmark Street remains the best place in London for independent music shops, particularly when it comes to guitars. Current occupants include **Regent Sounds** (no. 4, Fender and Gretsch guitar specialists, http://regentsounds.com) , **No.Tom** Vintage & Classic Guitars (no. 6, http://notomguitars.com), **Rose Morris** (no. 10, famous Rickenbacker guitar dealer, http://rosemorris.com) and the **Early Music Shop** (no. 11, the world's largest selection of medieval, renaissance and baroque musical instruments and sheet music, www.earlymusicshop.com).

Others include the **Music Room & Argents Printed Music** (no. 19, specialists in sheet music), **Wunjo Guitars** (no. 20, primarily guitars but also banjos, ukuleles, mandolins, keyboards, etc., www.wunjoguitars.com), **Denmark Street Studios** (no. 22, famous recording studio, http://denmarkstreetstudios.com), **Macaris** (no. 25, specialist in Gibson guitars, www.macaris.co.uk – with another store at 92-94 Charing Cross Rd) and **Denmark Street Guitars/Hanks Guitar Shop** (no. 27, over 3,000 instruments in stock, http://denmarkstreetonline.co.uk).

Denmark St, WC2 (Tottenham Court Rd tube).

Grahams Hi-Fi

Founded in 1929, Grahams is a specialist dealer in hi-fi products, home cinema and fully-integrated home entertainment systems; with over 85 years' experience, it's one of the world's leading hi-fi and TV shops. The store is situated mainly on one floor (with wheelchair access) and has four air-conditioned listening studios and free parking.

The Grahams' team spend a lot of time evaluating companies and products before choosing the equipment available on demonstration, and their brand list is a who's who of top names in the world of sound and vision, including Anthony Gallo, Arcam, B&W, Classe, Control, Creek, Crestron, Definitive Technology, Dynavector, Fuller Automation, Kaleidescape, Linn, Loewe, Lutron, M&K, Meridian, Naim, Neat, QED, Quadraspire, Rega, Ruckus, Sonos and Spendor.

Grahams also specialises in multi-room audio, lighting and heating control systems, and the installation of structured wiring for fully-integrated homes (including telephone, computers, television, cable, satellite and complete home control systems). Whether you wish to start 'modestly' with a new state-of-the-art hi-fi system or go all out for a more complex whole house automation system, Grahams provides solutions of the highest quality and standards.

Grahams Hi-Fi, 1 Canonbury Yard, 190A New North Rd, N1 7BS (020-7226 5500; www.grahams. co.uk; Essex Rd rail/Angel tube; Tue-Sat 9am-6pm, closed Sun-Mon).

Grays of Westminster

An award-winning camera shop, Grays of Westminster was founded over a quarter of a century ago by Gray Levett and is a shrine to the Nikon camera (it's the only brand on sale). The Pimlico store is unashamedly old world in style, with leather-topped desks and soft furnishings, although its cameras are state of the art.

It stocks the entire range of Nikon digital SLR cameras and accessories – the choice of the majority of professional photographers – and also has a vast array of secondhand equipment on display. Grays publish the biannual *Grays of Westminster Gazette*, which is essential reading among Nikon users.

Grays of Westminster, 40 Churton St, SW1V 2LP (020-7828 4925; www.graysofwestminster.co.uk; Pimlico tube; Mon-Fri 10am-5.30pm, Sat 10am-1pm, closed Sun).

HMV

Instantly recognisable by its iconic 'dog and gramophone' trademark, HMV (His Master's Voice) is synonymous with the history and development of British popular music and culture. It opened its first store on Oxford Street in 1921 and is a leading specialist retailer of music, film, games and technology products, with over 120 stores around the UK. In recent years, the company's fortunes have been hit hard by the digital music phenomenon, and in 2013 HMV was purchased by Hilco UK. The new owners closed HMV's flagship store at 150 Oxford Street – the largest music store in the world – and moved it back to its original site at 363 Oxford Street, albeit with a fresh new look.

HMV, 363 Oxford St, W1C 2LA (0843-221 0200; www.hmv.com/store-finder/hmv-oxford-street-363; Bond St tube; Mon-Sat 8am-9.30pm, Sun noon-6pm).

Honest Jon's

Founded by ('Honest') Jon Clare and Dave Ryner in 1974, Honest Jon's is a record shop on Portobello Road – one of London's best-known streets – and a musical institution. The shelves are packed with a multitude of musical genres, spanning jazz, blues, reggae, dance, disco, soul, folk, techno and world music, and it's a great place to browse rare vinyl. In 1992, the shop was taken over by Mark Ainley and Alan Sholefield – among the finest musicologists in the UK – who together with Blur frontman Damon Albarn set up Honest Jon's record label in 2002. The label specialises in international music, in keeping with the multicultural Portobello Rd vibe.

Honest Jon's, 278 Portobello Rd, W10 5TE (020-8969 9822; http://honestjons.com; Ladbroke Grove tube; Mon-Sat 10am-6pm, Sun 11am-5pm).

Jessops

Jessops was founded in Leicester in 1935 by Frank Jessop and was the UK's leading photographic retailer before going into administration in 2013. It was rescued by entrepreneur Peter Jones (of *Dragon's Den* fame), who re-launched the chain – there are now some 50 outlets across the UK.

The flagship store is on Oxford Street and personifies Jessops' reputation as a full-service photographic retailer, from hardware through to prints, offering a wide range of cameras, camcorders and accessories, including leading brands, which customers can engage with and experience at their leisure. The store also offers photography courses.

Jessops, 129-131 Oxford St, W1D 2HU (020-7434 3586; www.jessops.com; Tottenham Court Rd tube; Mon-Sat 9am-9pm, Sun 10am-6pm).

Kristina Records

A fixture on Stoke Newington Road in Dalston since 2011, Kristina Records attracts vinyl junkies from far and wide. It stocks a vast selection of new and used

vinyl across all genres – including some hard-to-find gems – particularly independent and underground music, cutting-edge house and techno, African, synth, reggae, vintage punk, disco, soul, new wave, pop and garage. If you're trying to track down a rare artist or LP, this is a great place to start. There's also an impressive section of brand new vinyl. Kristina's also buys and exchanges vinyl, from single records to entire collections.

Kristina Records, 44 Stoke Newington Rd, N16 7XJ (020-7254 2130; http://kristinarecords.com; Dalston Kingland rail; Mon, Wed-Fri noon-8pm, Sat 11am-8pm, Sun noon-6pm, closed Tue).

Maplin

Established in 1972 by Roger and Sandra Allen and Doug Simmons as a small mail-order business, Maplin is the UK's largest specialist retailer of consumer electronics. It offers a comprehensive range of over 15,000 products including audio/visual devices, electronics components, computer devices and peripherals, cables, television and satellite equipment, MP3 players, portable televisions and satellite navigation equipment, plus everyday electrical items such as batteries and light bulbs, power adaptors and solar energy panels.

Today it has more than 200 stores in the UK, with over 40 in the Greater London area, and its Great Portland Street store is an excellent resource for everyone from techies to novices.

Maplin, 6-10 Great Portland St, W1W 8QL (0333-400 9573; www.maplin.co.uk, Oxford Circus tube; Mon-Fri 9am-7pm, Sat 9am-6pm, Sun noon-6pm).

Oranges & Lemons

One of London's best hi-fi, home cinema and multi-room specialists for over 20 years, Oranges & Lemons in Battersea have built an enviable reputation for their expert advice and service. They offer a number

of comfortable listening rooms which are fully equipped to demonstrate, audition and compare a wide range of systems (using your favourite music or movies). As an independent and long-established store they have a privileged position in the industry and are able to cherry pick the finest audio and visual products from leading manufacturers, which include the cream of British firms as well

as the best products from North America and Japan.

O&L offers a full installation service, from delivering and connecting your hi-fi or home cinema kit to planning and specifying a full house multi-room system from scratch. If you're building a new home they will arrange a site visit to discuss exactly what you wish to achieve and then plan a system and draw up schematics for the correct cabling, working closely with your architect and electricians. Their engineers will install, configure and calibrate the system, and also ensure that you know how to operate it and get the most from it − and they're on call to troubleshoot any problems. That's service for you!

Oranges & Lemons, 61-63 Webb's Rd, SW11 6RX (020-7924 2040; www.oandlhifi.co.uk; Clapham S tube; Mon-Tue, Thu-Sat 10am-6pm, closed Wed, Sun).

Park Cameras

Founded in 1971 in Burgess Hill (West Sussex), Park Cameras waited more than 40 years to open a second store, but their London branch, just off Oxford Street, was worth the wait. Opened in 2013, it has more than 4,000ft^2 of browsing space, and is one of London's biggest and best camera stores. The first floor is dedicated to a wide range of cameras, camcorders and lenses from such big names as Canon, Fujifilm, Leica, Nikon, Olympus, Panasonic, Pentax, Samsung and Sony, while the ground floor houses an extensive choice of accessories including tripods, bags and other equipment. Truly a mecca for photography fans.

Park Cameras, 53-54 Rathbone Pl, W1T 1JR (020-7186 0007; www.parkcameras.com; Tottenham Court Rd tube; Mon-Wed, Sat 10am-6.30pm, Thu-Fri 10am-7.30pm, Sun 10am-4pm).

Phonica

Trading since 2003 when it was founded by Simon Rigg, Phonica is one of Soho's best-loved (and last) vinyl record shops. It offers the latest releases, pre-orders and merchandise, and is a honeypot for musicians and music lovers. The shop is also the storefront for the Vinyl Factory, one of the most famous independent record labels in London.

It's a one-stop-shop for authentic musical equipment and gifts, from turntables to musical literature, T-shirts to headphones and, of course, records – lots of them – from minimal to funk, downbeat to exotica. The staff really know their stuff and once they get to know your taste, they'll happily recommend records they think you'll like.

Phonica, 51 Poland St, W1F 7LZ (020-7025 6070; www.phonicarecords.com; Oxford Circus tube; Mon-Wed, Sat 11.30am-7.30pm, Thu-Fri 11.30am-8pm, Sun noon-6pm).

Rough Trade East

Although it was launched (in 2007) some 30 years after its parent store in Notting Hill, Rough Trade East – located in the iconic Old Truman Brewery on Brick Lane and encompassing 5,000ft^2 of sales space – is now the company's flagship store. It's primarily a retailer of vinyl (including exclusive releases), CDs and books, specialising in post-punk and other genres mostly within the alternative or underground scenes. The store also houses a café and a purpose-built stage, where free gigs and events are held in the evenings (there's standing room for around 200).

   Rough Trade declares its aims are 'to shorten the distance between artists and audiences, to faithfully represent the creativity and artistic talent of the music we recommend and sell'. It's one of the best places – if not **the** best – in the capital to stock up on music and attend live performances by new indie acts and cameos by audio leviathans such as Radiohead.

   There are other Rough Trade stores in Nottingham and, somewhat surprisingly, New York. In 1978, Rough Trade spawned Rough Trade Records, now an independent business, although links remain strong.

Rough Trade East, Dry Walk, Old Truman Brewery, 91 Brick Ln, E1 6QL (020-7392 7788; www.roughtrade.com; Shoreditch High St rail; Mon-Thu 8am-9pm, Fri 8am-8pm, Sat 10am-8pm, Sun 11am-7pm).

Suede

Yamaha

Starting life as Chappell of Bond Street – the original store was located at 50 New Bond Street, where Chappell had been trading since 1811 – Yamaha purchased the company in 2007, a year after it moved to Wardour Street. Rebranded as Yamaha Music London in 2013, it's Yamaha's European flagship store, occupying a Grade II listed property with three retail floors.

The store offers an impressive range of musical instruments including grand and upright pianos; acoustic, electric and classical guitars; keyboards, drums, brass, woodwind and string instruments: accessories, music production and PA equipment. There's also a treasure trove of over 50,000 sheet music books, and another 100,000 titles available to order. On the ground floor you'll find Yamaha's digital pianos and portable keyboards, plus the sheet music and orchestral instrument departments, while the first floor houses the famous piano hall, offering Yamaha, Bösendorfer and Kemble pianos. In the basement are guitars, drums and synthesisers, as well as pro audio and music production equipment.

There are regular in-store concerts, recitals and presentations (see website), which are usually free.

Yamaha Music London, 152-160 Wardour St, W1F 8YA (020-7432 4400; www.yamahamusiclondon. com; Tottenham Court Rd tube; Mon-Wed, Fri 9.30am-6pm, Thu 9.30am-8pm, Sat 10am-5.30pm, Sun 11am-5pm).

Liberty

4.
Department Stores

From Oxford Street to Knightsbridge via Bond Street, London is home to a roll-call of big-name department stores – once humble corner shops and now temples to the shopping gods. You can shop till you drop, get your hair and nails done, check out the latest fashions, furnish your home, stock your larder, pop into a pop-up (temporary concession), eat, drink and relax – all under one roof.

From the world-famous behemoths of Harrods and Selfridges – where you can buy everything from designer clothes to caviar and, in the case of Harrods, gold bars – to the fashionistas' favourites of Fenwick and Harvey Nicks, department stores are destinations in their own right for both locals and visitors. Other attractions include the world's most famous food emporium, Fortnum & Mason, and the fashion victims' honeypot, Dover Street Market. And if you're after the widest choice from a household name, the flagship stores of national chains such as John Lewis – the country's most popular department store – and perennial favourites Debenhams, House of Fraser and Marks & Spencer, can all be found in London.

Department stores also feature in the **Fashion (5)**, **Food & Drink (6)**, and **Furniture & Homeware (7)** chapters.

Debenhams

Founded in 1778 by William Clark – though named after William Debenham who became a partner in 1813 – the Debenhams department store chain has over 150 stores in the UK and Ireland, including the flagship store on Oxford Street. It may lack the luxurious feel of other West End stalwarts such as John Lewis and Selfridges but Debenhams has a loyal following and prides itself on being an affordable one-stop-shop for most retail needs, from fashion and beauty to homeware and electrical appliances.

Recently treated to a £25m makeover, Oxford Street does much to quash Debenhams' sometimes 'mumsy' image. It has seven floors and sells a wide range of clothes and shoes from British designers such as Jeff Banks, Jasper Conran, Henry Holland and Matthew Williamson – the store's 'Designers at Debenhams' brand

range has been a key ingredient since 1993. There's also a trendy homeware department and a vast beauty hall with an excellent range of the latest products and treatment rooms from the world's top cosmetics houses.

Should you need extra assistance or a refuelling stop, the store also offers wedding list, VIP baby and free personal shopper services, plus three in-store cafés and restaurants.

Debenhams, 334-348 Oxford St, W1C 1JG (0344-561 6161; www.debenhams.com/ newoxfordstreetstore; Bond St tube; Mon-Tue 9.30am-9pm, Wed-Sat 9.30am-10pm, Sun noon-6pm).

Dover Street Market

A hip store with an industrial warehouse vibe, über-cool Dover Street Market was founded by Comme des Garçons designer Rei Kawakubo and offers a novel approach to clothes shopping: it's a quirky, design-led store with an edgy street-market feel. But don't let the 'market' tag fool you as prices here aren't cheap. The store stocks rarefied labels such as Lanvin, Givenchy, Celine,

Azzedine Alaïa and Rick Owens, alongside the complete Comme des Garçons range in a seemingly ad hoc, constantly evolving space. Don't let the name fool you either, as DSM moved in March 2016 from Dover Street to the Grade II listed former Burberry building on Haymarket.

The store offers an original take on consumerism that combines a constantly evolving market atmosphere with avant-garde design. The minimalist, functional interior – with shop fittings made from raw and reclaimed materials such as shipping containers – provides a suitably stark backdrop for the many fashion designers, who are encouraged to adapt the space to suit their collection, making for a dynamic and unique interior.

While here take time out to visit the Rose Bakery, a classy café owned by Rose Carrarini, founder of the Villandry café-restaurant chain.

Dover Street Market, 18-22 Haymarket, SW1Y 4DG (020-7518 0680; http://london. doverstreetmarket.com; Piccadilly Circus tube; Mon-Sat 11am-7pm, Sun 11am-5pm).

Fenwick

Founded by John James Fenwick in 1882 in Newcastle-upon-Tyne (the Geordie city is still home to its HQ and flagship store), Fenwick is an independent chain of 11 department stores, including two in London (Bond Street and Brent Cross). Situated on the capital's most fashionable shopping street, the New Bond Street store opened in 1891; it doubled in size in 1980 to become the shop we see today. It's home to

five floors of luxury retail including designer clothing, homeware, bags, shoes, fashion, jewellery, perfume, cosmetics, cards, gifts and more.

If Harrods is the elder statesman of department stores, Fenwick is the eccentric aunt. The ground floor is crammed with accessories including luxury headscarves and fascinators, knitwear, leather bags, hats, lingerie, hosiery and an excellent perfume department. It stocks a good range

of offbeat, slightly bohemian British design, ranging from Orla Kiely accessories to Tallulah and Hope kaftans, while elsewhere the store has modernised in recent years to include a new suite of contemporary designers.

There's also a range of beauty services including a spa, massage, facials, nail bar and hair salon, and when you need a break from splashing the cash there's Carluccio's Italian eatery and its Bond & Brook restaurant and bar.

Fenwick, 63 New Bond St, W1S 1RQ (020-7629 9161; www.fenwick.co.uk/stores/bond-street; Bond St tube; Mon-Wed, Fri-Sat 10am-7.30pm, Thu 10am-8pm, Sun noon-6pm).

Fortnum & Mason

Fortnum & Mason (usually referred to simply as 'Fortnums') on Piccadilly is one of Britain's oldest department stores, established in 1707 by William Fortnum and Hugh Mason. The store underwent a £24 million refurbishment in 2007 as part of its tercentenary celebrations and is on most foodies' must-visit list.

Founded as a grocery store, its reputation was built on supplying top-quality food, and its fame grew rapidly throughout the Victorian era. Over the years it developed into a department store, although Fortnums' reputation rests largely on its food hall which is situated on the lower ground and ground floors. Not the place to do your weekly shop – unless your surname happens to be Windsor – but wonderful for the occasional treat.

Today Fortnums is recognised internationally as a British icon, proudly displaying its royal warrant above the door (it's dubbed the 'Queen's grocer'), and is a compelling combination of delicatessen, department store, restaurant and living museum. In addition to the food hall there's homeware on the first floor; the second floor is home to beauty rooms, fashion accessories, jewellery and a perfumery; while the third floor has menswear, luggage and writing accessories, along with an excellent wrapping service. There are also a celebrated tea shop and no fewer than five restaurants.

Fortnum & Mason, 181 Piccadilly, W1A 1ER (020-7734 8040; www.fortnumandmason.com; Green Pk/Piccadilly tube; Mon-Sat 10am-8pm, Sun noon-6pm).

Harrods

Founded in 1834, Harrods in Knightsbridge is the world's most famous department store and a British institution, even though it's owned by Qatar Holdings who paid £1.5 billion for it in 2010. It's also one of the world's largest stores, extending

to 4.5 acres (1.82ha), with more than 1 million ft² (305,000m²) of selling space over seven floors divided into some 330 departments. Harrods is said to be able to provide anything a customer wants: its motto is *Omnia Omnibus Ubique* (All Things for All People, Everywhere) and its clientele is decidedly upmarket.

Harrods astonishes and intrigues in equal measure with its first-class service, retail theatre and product quality, not to mention an unmatched international brand selection. From its humble beginnings as a grocer,

it has become a Terracotta Palace crammed with luxury merchandise from bags to beds, haute couture to homeware, pianos to pet accessories, plus a selection of premier services such as 'by appointment' personal shopping, Harrods bank and gold bullion.

Its pièce de résistance is its celebrated Art Nouveau food hall (above), where the majestic décor provides a glorious backdrop for the artful displays of food, notable for its variety, quality and luxury – and eye-watering prices! There are also some 30 restaurants and food outlets serving everything from frozen yogurt to oysters.

Harrods, 87-135 Brompton Rd, SW1X 7XL (020-7730 1234; www.harrods.com; Knightsbridge tube; Mon-Sat 10am-9pm, Sun noon-6pm).

Harvey Nichols

The younger, more fashionable cousin of Harrods, Harvey Nichols (dubbed 'Harvey Nicks') was founded in 1813 as a linen shop and has grown into a nationwide chain of prestigious department stores: its

original flagship store is in Knightsbridge, with others in Birmingham, Bristol, Dublin, Edinburgh, Leeds, Liverpool and Manchester (plus a number overseas). Harvey Nicks is often compared with Harrods (just a stone's throw away), but while Harrods offers huge variety across a massive range of products, HN concentrates on designer clothes, homeware and food, as well as the obligatory beauty department. The store is best known for its fashionable clothes and accessories – it stocks many of the world's most prestigious brands – and attracts a younger clientele than Harrods, which tends to be more upmarket. The fifth-floor Foodmarket boasts over 600 exclusive products in Harvey Nicks' smart black and silver livery, along with some pretty luxurious foodie treats and accessories, from gin and tonic popcorn to a champagne sabre (£99.95).

The store's celebrated restaurant, bar and café have become destinations in their own right and are favourite meeting places for savvy shoppers.

Harvey Nichols, 109-125 Knightsbridge, SW1X 7RJ (020-7235 5000; www.harveynichols.com/store/knightsbridge; Knightsbridge tube; Mon-Sat 10am-8pm, Sun noon-6pm).

House of Fraser

Founded as a small drapery shop by Hugh Fraser in Glasgow in 1849, House of Fraser (known to its fans as HoF) is one of the best-known names on Oxford Street. It

occupies the building that once housed D H Evans, which HoF acquired in 1959, and is renowned for its designer brands and exclusive collections, beauty hall and homeware department. The flagship Oxford Street store is part of a chain of over 60 UK stores which includes outlets at London City (opposite London Bridge), Victoria, Westfield Shopping Centre in west London, and Richmond.

HoF prides itself on selling luxury goods at affordable prices and stocks a wide range of designer brands – including exclusive lines – and own label goods. Whether you're looking for fashion, accessories, cosmetics, luggage, gifts or toys, you'll find it here.

One of the highlights in 2016 included a new range from iconic Irish fashion designer Helen McAlinden, whose contemporary cuts are designed for classic dressers who like a modern twist.

For the perfect day out you can have a shopping session with an in-store personal stylist, relax in the Clarins Spa, followed by lunch or afternoon tea in the Café Zest restaurant.

House of Fraser, 318 Oxford St, W1C 1HF (0344-800 3752; www.houseoffraser.co.uk; Bond St/ Oxford Circus tube; Mon-Sat 9.30am-9pm, Sun noon-6.30pm).

John Lewis

Britain's most beloved store, John Lewis frequently tops surveys of the most popular UK retailers and scores highly on its quality own-brand products and excellent customer service. It offers solid good value (its motto is 'never knowingly undersold'), an unconditional returns policy, and a general feeling of good taste rather than showy fashion.

The launch of its Christmas TV advert has become an annual event.

Founded by John Spedan Lewis in 1864, the store has grown from a humble drapery shop to a mighty chain of some 46 stores. One of the most unusual aspects of the John Lewis Partnership – which also owns Peter Jones (see page 80) and the Waitrose supermarket chain – is that it's a limited public company that's held in trust on behalf of its over 90,000 employees or 'partners', all of whom receive an annual share of the profits.

The Oxford Street branch is its undoubted flagship. It boasts some 20 departments over seven floors, including fashion, beauty, fabrics, homeware, kitchen, electrical goods, toiletries, toys and technology products, along with a splendid Waitrose food hall on the lower ground floor. There's also a coffee shop and a restaurant, plus various fast food outlets.

John Lewis, 300 Oxford St, W1C 1EX (020-7629 7711; www.johnlewis.com/our-shops/oxford-street; Oxford Circus tube; Mon-Wed, Fri-Sat 9.30am-8pm, Thu 9.30am-9pm, Sun noon-6pm).

Liberty

Synonymous with luxury and outstanding design since its launch in 1875, Liberty is one of London's must-visit stores. Arthur Lasenby Liberty's intuitive vision and pioneering spirit led him to travel the world seeking individual pieces to inspire

and excite his discerning clientele. Thus Liberty isn't just a name above the door, but Arthur Liberty's legacy, which stands for integrity, value, quality and, above all, beautiful design – not least the timber-framed, mock-Tudor store built in 1924. (The Liberty staircases are designed in such an odd way that customers often get lost, which led to the publication – in the '70s – of a free booklet entitled 'How Not to Get Lost in Liberty's'!)

Liberty has a long history of artistic and inspiring collaborative projects, from

William Morris and Gabriel Dante Rossetti in the 19th century to Yves Saint Laurent, Mary Quant and Dame Vivienne Westwood in the 20th century. Recent collaborations include renowned brands such as Nike, Kate Moss for Topshop, Hermes and Manolo Blahnik, to name but a few. Nowadays Liberty sells fashions, cosmetics, haberdashery, fabrics, accessories and gifts, in addition to its unique homeware and furniture. When you've soaked up the atmosphere, take a break in the excellent café/restaurant on the second floor.

Unapologetically eccentric and truly innovative, Liberty is a London icon.

Liberty, Regent St, W1B 5AH (020-7734 1234; www.liberty.co.uk; Oxford Circus/Piccadilly Circus tube; Mon-Sat 10am-8pm, Sun noon-6pm).

Marks & Spencer

When Michael Marks and Thomas Spencer set up their penny bazaar market stall in Leeds in 1884 they could never have guessed they were launching one of the UK's retail giants. Marks & Spencer (variously known as M&S, Marks and Sparks or simply Marks) is now one of Britain's largest chains with some 350 UK department stores (or over 800 if you include the smaller Simply Food convenience stores). It's a British institution with a reputation for high-quality products and excellent customer service, specialising in clothing, homeware and food.

M&S is the UK's largest clothing retailer. It has struggled in recent years, although its lingerie remains popular and most British women own at least some items of M&S underwear. It's also a multi-billion pound food retailer, and although its food range is more limited and expensive than most stores, it offers high quality and reliability. It also sells homeware such as bed linen, but this is a smaller part of the business than the other two ranges.

London's flagship M&S store at Marble Arch boasts an impressive range of affordable buys, with staples such as lingerie and clothing joined by flowers and gifts, beauty products, home accessories, furniture and furnishings. There's also an impressive food hall and a café when you need a break.

Marks & Spencer, 458 Oxford St, W1C 1AP (020-7935 7954; www.marksandspencer.com; Marble Arch tube; Mon-Sat 9am-9pm, Sun noon-6pm).

Peter Jones

Like many of London's iconic department stores, Peter Jones began (in 1877) as a one-man draper's shop. Founded by Welshman Peter Rees Jones, he expanded the business over the years until it covered most of the block overlooking Sloane Square. On Jones' death in 1905, the store was purchased by John Lewis (see page 77), who, out of respect for its founder, retained its original name and didn't absorb into the John Lewis brand.

One of the largest and best-loved department stores in London, Peter Jones (known affectionately as PJs to its fans) occupies an eye-catching building which was built in the '30s. Grade II* listed, it demonstrates the first modern-movement use of a glass curtain wall in Britain and following a £100 million refit in 2004 it remains one of London's most dramatic stores with six tiers of curved glass balconies.

There's an air of exclusivity about PJs – the spiritual home of the Sloane Rangers – although its stock and décor are no different from any other John Lewis store, with departments encompassing men's and women's fashion, beauty, home and garden, electricals, gifts, toys, sports and leisure, and more. When you need a break there's an espresso bar and two restaurants.

Peter Jones, Sloane Sq, SW1W 8EL (020-7730 3434; www.johnlewis.com/our-shops/peter-jones; Sloane Sq tube; Mon-Tue, Thu-Sat 9.30am-7pm, Wed 9.30am-8pm, Sun noon-6pm).

Selfridges

The man who's said to have coined the phrase 'the customer is always right', American entrepreneur Harry Gordon Selfridge was a pioneer of department store retailing. His story sparked *Mr Selfridge*, a BBC drama series running since 2013, while his legacy has been a small but influential chain of department stores including one in Birmingham, two in Manchester and the original flagship store on Oxford Street which opened in 1909.

The second-largest store in the UK after Harrods (see page 74), Selfridges offers one of the most exciting and fashionable shopping experiences in London. Whatever you're after – clothes, bags, shoes, cosmetics, soft furnishings, books, kitchenware, artisan food, etc. – you'll find it in Selfridges. With its concession boutiques, store-wide themed events and collections from the hottest new brands, it's the first

port-of-call for stylish one-stop shopping, while useful floor plans make navigating the store simplicity itself.

If it's luxury you desire, visit the Wonder Room on the ground floor: 19,000ft^2 of exclusive brands, with stunning collections of jewellery and watches from the likes of Bulgari, Cartier and Tiffany. And when you need a break there's a huge choice of great eating places, including a variety of restaurants, cafés, bars and fast-food concessions.

Selfridges, 400 Oxford St, W1A 1AB (0800-123400; www.selfridges.com/london; Bond St tube; Mon-Sat 9.30am-9pm, Sun 11.30am-6pm).

& Other Stories

5.
Fashion

When it comes to fashion, London breaks the rules like nowhere else. The city is synonymous with cutting-edge style and is one of the world's leading fashion centres, offering everything from handmade shoes and bespoke tailoring to 'fast fashion', grunge and vintage. What London lacks in haute couture houses, it more than makes up for by the sheer variety, energy and innovation of its fashion scene.

We have concentrated on indie boutiques rather than high-street chains and luxury labels, although we couldn't fail to include the major department stores – which are in the fashion vanguard – and a few noteworthy megastores. For years the city has garnered a wealth of avant-garde boutiques carrying the most stylish designers and cult brands, both British and international, and in recent times a new wave of lifestyle boutiques and concept stores have burst onto the scene.

The city's best fashion boutiques are no longer confined to the West End and nowadays fashionistas are just as likely to buy their gear in Hoxton or Notting Hill as Bond Street or Knightsbridge.

Price guide: £ = budget, ££ = superior, £££ = designer

& Other Stories

H&M's 'luxury' chain opened its flagship store for women's ready-to-wear and accessories in 2013 and has been a fashion favourite ever since, largely due to their track record for producing mid-range 'wardrobe treasures' at high street prices.

Drop in to see their latest collaborations with international designers – a recent example was a line co-created with Rodarte for Spring-Summer 2016 – and stay to check out the store's catwalk-inspired prints, affordable silk, suede and cashmere, and cult new brands and colours at the beauty counter. A Swedish shopping sensation for those with champagne tastes on a prosecco budget.

& Other Stories, 256-258 Regent St, W1B 3AF (020-3402 9190; www.stories.com; Oxford St tube; Mon-Fri 10am-9pm, Sat 10am-8pm, Sun noon-6pm; £).

69b Broadway Market

Founded in 2011 by former fashion editor and stylist Merryn Leslie, 69b is a women's sustainable fashion outlet on

Broadway Market in Hackney. The shop stocks an exclusive and contemporary range of established and up-and-coming British and international brands – such as People Tree, Beaumont Organic and Ancient Greek Sandals – all of which are committed to sustainable practices and philosophy.

Leslie believes in complete transparency, from laboratory or farm to designer, producer and consumer. All her designers are environmentally conscious and driven, employ craftsmen who uphold traditional techniques, and are constantly seeking ways to reduce their environmental impact.

69b Broadway Market, E8 4PH (020-7249 9655; www.69bboutique.com; London Fields rail; Mon-Fri 10.30am-6.30pm, Sat 10am-6pm, Sun 11am-6pm; £-££).

Aimé

Fashion and lifestyle emporium Aimé was started by French Cambodian sisters Val and Vanda Heng Vong, who while studying in London in 1999 missed their favourite Parisian labels and products and had the inspired idea to open their own boutique.

The stock has widened from French names such as Isabel Marant Étoile, Antik Batik, Les Prairies de Paris, APC and Repetto, to include Spanish designer Masscob and Italian houses Forte Forte and Faliero Sarti (among others). The shop also offers a range of brands for babies and children (e.g. Soeur), plus jewellery and fragrances. There's another branch on trendy Redchurch Street in Shoreditch.

Aimé, 32 Ledbury Rd, W11 2AB (020-7221 7070; www.aimelondon.com; Notting Hill Gate tube; Mon-Sat 10am-6.30pm, closed Sun; ££-£££).

Albam

Opened in 2006 by James Shaw and Alastair Rae, menswear shop Albam now has three London outlets; the original on Beak Street and others in Islington and Spitalfields. Albam designs practical and sophisticated menswear with an attention to detail and production quality that are refreshing in the world of fast fashion. From the outset it has endeavoured to create pieces that customers really value: timeless, functional wardrobe staples where the details and finishing are key. The company's philosophy is to produce 'modern crafted clothing' using, wherever possible, British suppliers and manufacturers.

The Beak Street store showcases the full Albam menswear collection alongside a small selection of other brands.

Albam, 23 Beak St, W1F 9RS (020-3157 7000; www.albamclothing.com; Oxford Circus tube; Mon-Sat 11am-7pm, Sun noon-5.30pm; £-££).

Alexander Wang

Journalists might have expected this edgy designer to open his London store in the East End, but the site Wang chose instead was a coup. His Mayfair flagship occupies three floors of the old post office – big enough to stock something from every category, whether key rings or Bretons from the 'T' range, or silk and leather pieces off the runway (available in-store only).

The stone and rubber-clad venue is an unmissable stop-off for anyone with an interest in seeing the latest designer palace. Its design amplifies the uncompromising aesthetic that has made Wang such a big influence on fashion and such an exciting prospect since leaving Balenciaga to go it alone.

Alexander Wang, 43-44 Albemarle St, W1S 4JJ (020-3727 5568; www.alexanderwang.com; Oxford Circus tube; Mon-Sat 11am-7pm, Sun noon-6pm; £££).

Ally Capellino

Opened in 2005 by Alison Lloyd, Ally Capellino produces a wide range of elegant bags – satchels, totes, rucksacks, clutches, travel bags, etc. – for both men and women, alongside a range of fashion accessories such as belts, wallets and scarves. Her signature pieces include understated unisex satchels made from waxed cotton or canvas with leather buckles, crisp canvas beach bags with rope handles, and simple handbags with brass frames and buffalo leather detailing.

British manufacturing, timeless styling, attention to detail and a unique mix of quirk and quality ensure Ally Capellino has a host of fans. There are other outlets in Marylebone and Portobello Road.

Ally Capellino, 9 Calvert Ave, E2 7JP (020-7033 7843; www.allycapellino.co.uk; Shoreditch High St rail; Mon-Sat 11am-6pm, Sun 11am-5pm; ££-£££).

Anna

Opened in 1997, Anna Park's flagship boutique in Primrose Hill is part of a small chain of six shops – and the only one in London – which make up one of the UK's largest and most successful independent womenswear retailers. Spread over two floors, the store offers a winning combination of beautiful clothes and accessories from a vast array of national and international labels plus exemplary customer service, offering customers personal one-on-one style advice.

A wealth of design talent is sourced and promoted within the store in order to maintain its fresh innovative style and keep its ever-expanding customer base happy.

Anna, 126 Regent's Park Rd, NW1 8XL (020-7483 0411; www.shopatanna.com; Chalk Farm tube; Mon-Sat 10am-6pm, Sun noon-6pm; ££-£££).

Anya Hindmarch

Launched in London in 1987, Anya Hindmarch's leather goods business has grown into a global brand with over 45 branches worldwide, including flagship stores in London, New York and Tokyo. There are also five Bespoke stores, including one in Pont Street in London (see http://anyasworld.anyahindmarch.com/bespoke) where you can have drawings or messages in your own handwriting embossed onto items by in-store craftsmen.

Anya is a passionate advocate of British design and arts, and her beautiful products embody the finest materials, superb craftsmanship and exquisite design, and are objects of lust among fashionistas. She regularly receives awards, including (most recently) Accessories Designer of the Year at the 2014 British Fashion Awards and 2016 *Elle* Style Awards, and *Glamour* magazine's Designer of the Year (2015).

Anya Hindmarch, 118 New Bond St, W1S 1EW (020-7493 1628; www.anyahindmarch.com; Bond St tube; Mon-Wed, Fri-Sat 10am-6.30pm, Thu 10am-7pm, Sun noon-5pm; £££).

Atsuko Kudo

Founded in 2000, Atsuko Kudo designs and manufactures a full range of womenswear (and a few items for men) made exclusively in latex rubber, inspired by the dark glamour of the mid-20th century – from Hollywood's fascination with 'noir' and European couture through to Dior's transformative elegance in the post-war years.

All garments and accessories are available in a wide variety of plain colours and uniquely patterned prints, from individual garments to complete ensembles – for the bedroom, the salon, the nightclub or any other occasion – and not just for those with a body like Kim Kardashian…

Atsuko Kudo, 64 Holloway Rd, N7 8JL (020-7697 9072; www.atsukokudo.com; Highbury & Islington tube; Mon-Sat 10.30am-7pm, closed Sun; ££-£££).

Bernstock Speirs

Established in 1982 by Paul Bernstock and Thelma Speirs, who met whilst studying Fashion and Textiles at Middlesex University, avant-garde Bernstock Speirs create men's and women's hats that challenge the traditional ideas of millinery. After over 30 years in business the brand remains vibrant and fresh, with new generations of hat wearers seduced by the witty and innovative styles and exceptional quality.

From felt fedoras adorned with inky feathers to feminine baseball caps with satin bows, and midnight blue felt trilbys to hybrid beanie/fascinators, Bernstock Speirs' hats are playful, fashionable and beautifully crafted in premium and unconventional materials.

Bernstock Speirs, 234 Brick Ln, E2 7EB (020-7739 7385; www.bernstockspeirs.com; Shoreditch High St rail; Mon-Sat 10am-6pm, closed Sun; ££).

Blackout II

One of London's best vintage stores, trading in the heart of Covent Garden for some 30 years, Blackout offers two floors of vintage (from the '20s to the '80s) threads and accessories for men and women. Selling quirky vintage clothing long before retro gear became hip, the store is an Aladdin's cave, offering a wealth of cool dresses from the '20s and '30s, as well as more wearable men's and womenswear from the '40s through to the '80s. There's also a wide range of accessories, costume jewellery, hats, handbags and shoes.

You can also hire outfits for special occasions. Not the cheapest around, but the range is fantastic.

Blackout II, 51 Endell St, WC2H 9AJ (020-7240 5006; www.blackout2.com; Covent Gdn tube; Mon-Fri 11am-7pm, Sat 11.30am-6.30pm, closed Sun; £-££).

Blitz

More of a vintage department store – occupying five rooms over two floors of an old warehouse – Blitz is London's (and Europe's) largest vintage store with over 20,000 unique pieces. The vast stock includes men's and women's fashion, shoes and accessories from the '60s to the '90s, plus millennial trends; it also has a huge collection of genuine designer vintage stock, including everything from Biba to McQueen.

And it isn't just clothes and designer chic, Blitz is a one-stop shop for all things vintage, including accessories, luggage, posters, watches, bikes, furniture and more – and there's also a mini book store and café (great cannoli!).

Blitz, 55-59 Hanbury St, E1 5JP (020-7377 0730; www.blitzlondon.co.uk; Shoreditch High St rail; Mon-Sat 11am-7pm, Sun noon-6pm; £-££).

British Red Cross Chelsea

This British Red Cross shop isn't your run-of-the-mill charity shop, but rather an outlet for 'pre-owned' designer clobber that offers a rewarding hunting ground for bargain-hunting fashionistas. Not surprisingly, it's Chelsea's most popular charity shop, where the area's well-heeled

residents off-load last season's wardrobe. It bills itself as a 'designer charity shop' (clothes, shoes, bags and accessories), specialising in designer and quality vintage – you might even find some haute-couture. Prices are based on the original cost, so they aren't a steal but are still great value.

The shop also organises special 'designer' and 'vintage' evenings – ask to be added to the guest list.

British Red Cross Chelsea, 69-71 Old Church St, SW3 5BS (020-7376 7300; www.redcross.org.uk; S Kensington tube; Mon-Sat 10am-6pm, closed Sun; ££).

Browns

What started in 1970 as a small boutique housed on the ground floor at 27 South Molton Street has expanded to take over five adjoining townhouses. Today, Browns – owned by Joan Burstein and her husband Sidney – is a legend and one of the city's top fashion destinations, offering women and men (no. 23 caters exclusively for men) ready-to-wear and accessories for every occasion.

Joan Burstein is credited with discovering such talents as John Galliano, Alexander McQueen, Hussein Chalayan and Commes des Garcons. One of London's most celebrated fashion landmarks, Browns continues to offer stunning creations hand-picked from the world's top designers. Reassuringly expensive!

Browns, 24-27 South Molton St, W1K 5RD (020-7514 0016; www.brownsfashion.com; Bond St tube; Mon-Wed, Sat 10am-7pm, Thu-Fri 10am-8pm, Sun noon-6pm; £££).

Celestine Eleven

A vast fashion emporium and holistic treatment centre founded by Tena Strok, Celestine Eleven is a concept store – polished concrete, zinc counters and quirky furniture – offering a wealth of beautiful clothes. With its focus on pure living and elegant style brands, it's the sort of boutique you'd expect to see in west London rather than Shoreditch, stocking fashionable young designers and cult beauty products. Strok is a former stylist, and rather than fill her shop with sure-fire sellers such as Mulberry bags, she has sourced interesting labels from London, Paris and Scandinavia.

When you're done splashing the cash, you can join a yoga class in the studio downstairs.

Celestine Eleven, 4 Holywell Ln, EC2A 3ET (020-7729 2987; www.celestineeleven.com; Shoreditch High St rail; Mon-Sat 11am-7pm, Sun noon-5pm; ££-£££).

Céline

F rench luxury ready-to-wear and leather goods brand Céline was founded in 1945 by Céline Vipiana, and has been owned by the LVMH (Louis Vuitton Moët Hennessy) group since 1996. Offering elegant Parisian designs for stylish women, particularly those with a passion for luxury leather, the vast Mount Street flagship store presents the whole collection of Céline designs.

Designed by creative director Phoebe Philo, the interior boasts a strikingly beautiful patchwork of some 6,000 marble tiles inlaid with semi-precious stones. It's complemented by bespoke fittings by Dutch artist Thomas Poulsen, such as the huge brass lights that spread their spider-like limbs over the central atrium. Young, sexy, beautiful – and very expensive.

Céline, 103 Mount St, W1K 2AP (020-7491 8200; www.celine.com; Bond St tube; Mon-Sat 10am-6.30pm, closed Sun; £££).

Couverture & the Garbstore

A cult high-end designer fashion and homeware store in Notting Hill, Couverture & the Garbstore is actually two shops in one: the Garbstore serves up designer and vintage fashion, while Couverture offers an eclectic mix of homeware and beauty products. The store is arranged over three floors, with the lower ground floor dedicated to Ian Paley's menswear brand, Garbstore. The ground and galleried first floors are dedicated to the Couverture collections, which include womenswear and accessories, children's clothes and baby gear, toys, jewellery, home accessories, ceramics, furniture and covetable vintage finds.

A great place to browse, even if you aren't planning to buy.

Couverture & The Garbstore, 188 Kensington Park Rd, W11 2ES (020-7229 2178; http:// couvertureandthegarbstore.com; Ladbroke Grove tube; Mon-Sat 10am-6pm, Sun noon-5pm; ££).

J. Crew

A merican super-brand J. Crew's vast flagship store on Regent Street – its first outside the US and one of several in the capital – spans two floors and runs to over 17,000ft^2. Housing their complete collection of womenswear, menswear and children's wear, this cool store resembles a period townhouse with wooden floors, antique furniture and a curated art collection.

The company has been making its colourful preppy clothing since 1983; conceived in its New York City design studio, J. Crew's clothes are noted for their clever design, timeless appeal and superb quality. A great place to shop, whether you're looking for basics or a stand-out party piece.

J. Crew, 165 Regent St, W1B 4AD (020-7292 1580; www.jcrew.com; Oxford Circus tube; Mon-Sat 10am-8pm, Sun noon-6pm; ££).

The Cross

One of London's first 'lifestyle' boutiques, The Cross was opened by Sam Robinson in 1996, since when the city's fashionistas have been beating a path to its door. Offering an eclectic mix of women's fashion, kidswear, homeware and gifts, it's a unique and charming shopping destination, tucked away in an idyllic tree-lined street in Holland Park.

The Cross stocks often hard-to-find fashion labels such as Dosa, English Weather, Forte Forte, Mes Desmoiselles, Pomandere, Samantha Sung, Velvet by Graham & Spencer and Zero + Maria Cornejo, to name just a few. There are also unique homeware and textiles by Loaf Lifestyle, Nathalie Lete, Shirley McLauchlan and Suzusan, alongside rare vintage and global finds.

The Cross, 141 Portland Rd, W11 4LR (020-7727 6760; www.thecrossshop.co.uk; Holland Pk tube; Mon-Sat 10am-6pm, closed Sun; ££-£££).

Darkroom

Located in fashionable Lamb's Conduit Street in Bloomsbury, Darkroom is a concept store specialising in unique and hard-to-find accessories, offering an eclectic mix of handmade goodies for men, women and the home, including bold jewellery, *objets d'art*, graphic prints, textiles, stationery, homeware, soft furnishings, leather goods, bags and more.

Darkroom champions emerging and undiscovered global designers and artisans (such as London studio Uribe, Belgian designer Georges Larondelle and *Vogue*-featured Noemi Klein) to assemble its range of exclusive items, special commissions and their in-house Darkroom collections, celebrating craftsmanship, colour and texture. A visit to Darkroom encourages lingering, getting lost and discovering something new…

Darkroom, 52 Lamb's Conduit St, WC1N 3LL (020-7831 7244; https://darkroomlondon.com; Russell Sq tube; Mon-Fri 11am-7pm, Sat 11am-6pm, Sun noon-5pm; £-££).

Department Stores

London's department stores (see **Chapter 4**) are famous for their fashion departments, offering everything from affordable everyday basics to luxury accessories and exclusive designer frocks to timeless staples (for both men and women). Many leading boutiques, designers and high street names are represented in department stores, which allow you to compare clothes across a wealth of designers, styles and prices all under one roof.

Debenhams: Debenhams gives its customers a unique, differentiated and exclusive mix of own brands, international houses and concessions. It has been investing in design for over 20 years through its exclusive 'Designers at Debenhams' portfolio that includes the likes of Ben de Lisi, Betty Jackson, Sadie Frost and Jemima French, Henry Holland, Janet Reger, Jasper

Conran, Jeff Banks, John Rocha, Julien Macdonald, Matthew Williamson, Patrick Grant and Savannah Miller. Affordable fashion for the masses. (£)

Dover Street Market: Comme des Garçons designer Rei Kawakubo's groundbreaking Dover Street Market is super-cool, combining the dynamic energy of London's indoor markets with established fashion brands for both men and women. All the Comme collections are here, alongside exclusive lines such as Valentino, Givenchy and Azzedine Alaïa, and areas devoted

to Céline, Saint Lauren and Rick Owens to name just a few. NB: it may be called a 'market' but this is no place for bargaining or bargains, with prices as exclusive as the fashions on offer. (£££)

Fenwick: A key destination for fashion cognoscenti with quirky, fledgling labels sitting alongside international designers, Fenwick appeals to grown-up women and men who value quality over fast fashion. Among the artfully chosen selection of niche brands are clothes by everyday designers such as L K Bennett and Orla Kiely with more exclusive names like Max Mara, Nicole Farhi and Joseph on the second floor, and jeans and casualwear at the very top. On the ground floor you can browse through luxury scarves, knitwear, leather bags, jewellery, lingerie and accessories. A bijou department store bursting at the seams with head-turning outfits. (££-£££)

Harrods: You can buy virtually anything at Harrods, although it's on the fashion and beauty fronts that this iconic store really comes into its own. From its well-edited heavyweight collections in the Superbrands department and Designer Studio on the first floor, to the stunning Shoe Heaven on the fifth floor and the huge menswear department on the lower ground floor, Harrods has it all. Everything sold here is branded, either made for Harrods' own house brand or from famous international fashion houses such as Louis Vuitton, Hermès, YSL, Gucci, Hugo Boss, Giorgio Armani, Versace et al. (£££)

Harrods' legendary summer and winter sales are must-visit events with some great deals, provided you're up for doing battle with the hordes of bargain hunters.

Harvey Nichols: A must for fashionistas, the store brings together an impressive range of designers from around the world and supplies its elite clientele with fine clothes (Alexander McQueen, Comme des Garçons, D&G, John Galliano, Space NK, Burberry, Jimmy Choo and Versace), as well as accessories, cosmetics, food and shoes. Be sure to make the most of your time by calling on the in-store stylists and concierge if you feel the need. (££-£££)

House of Fraser: One of the best-known names on Oxford Street, House of Fraser (HoF) is renowned for its designer brands and exclusive own-label collections, and prides itself on selling affordable luxury whatever your budget; clothes that are a bit edgy, fun and good quality, including names such as Levi's, Pied A Terre, Whistles, J Brand and Barbour.

One of the 2016 highlights included a new range from iconic Irish fashion designer Helen McAlinden, whose contemporary cuts are designed for classic dressers who yearn for a modern twist. Whether you're seeking fashion, accessories, cosmetics, luggage, gifts or toys, you'll find it here. (£-££)

John Lewis: Britain's favourite store, John Lewis has increased its market share of clothing sales in recent years. Once associated with sensible knitwear and cosy slippers, the 40-plus store chain has polished its fashion credentials through designer collaborations, classy own-label products (great value cashmere) and the addition of upmarket brands that had previously steered clear of the store.

John Lewis' fashion floors now mix the likes of Jaeger, Hobbs, Mango and Whistles

with smaller labels such as Coast, Toast and Fenn Wright Manson. Prices can stretch up to Ralph Lauren levels but also include beloved British brands such as Alice Temperley's Somerset and the cheaper Kin. (£-£££)

Liberty: It may be one of London's most traditional stores – synonymous with iconic design and craftsmanship since 1874 – but venture inside Liberty and you'll find a whole host of great clothes from the best of the British design industry. Not content with merely following trends, Liberty regularly showcases and sponsors new designers,

offering cutting-edge style with names such as Martin Margiela and Comme des Garçons nestling alongside

Liberty has a history of collaborative projects – from William Morris and Gabriel Dante Rossetti in the 19th century to Yves Saint Laurent and Dame Vivienne Westwood in the 20th.

Betty Jackson, Vivienne Westwood, Chloé and Tod's. Recent collaborations have included lines with Nike, Jimmy Choo, Kate Moss, Hermès, Manolo Blahnik and Uniqlo, to name but a few. A fashionista's dream. (££-£££)

Marks & Spencer: Long synonymous with good quality and value for money (not to mention sustainability), M&S is the UK's largest clothing retailer and has been a high-street favourite for over a century. In recent years it has had success with its Autograph (where famous fashion designers are hired to collaborate on collections, such as an Alexa Chung collection and Rosie Huntingdon-Whiteley lingerie in 2016) and Per Una ranges, but has fallen behind its young and thrusting high-street rivals.

Some industry analysts think that M&S should concentrate on what it does best – staples such as knitwear, cashmere

and lingerie – rather than trying to cater to everyone's tastes. Nevertheless, many women (and men) don't realise just how much good stuff there still is in M&S – at least in its flagship London stores. (£)

Peter Jones: One of London's most popular department stores, PJs manages to keep up with today's fashions and tastes, with its exclusive, chic appeal that's only fitting for the modish King's Road location.

Although traditionally a draw for the 'mature' woman, nowadays it attracts a more youthful clientele to its dazzling accessories section and concessions dedicated to familiar fashion names such as Warehouse, Coast and Hobbs. Struggling to choose? Get a free consultation from a fashion advisor to help achieve the look you want, which you can then complete in-house with stunning shoes, jewellery and handbags. (£-£££)

Selfridges: With its concession boutiques, store-wide themed events and collections from the hottest new brands, Selfridges is often the first port-of-call for stylish one-stop shopping, and one of the most exciting places to shop in the capital.

Selfridges is known for its noteworthy concessions, such as Polish girl brand Local Heroes and new sports luxe label This Is A Love Song.

The store offers some of the world's most exclusive designer clothes, but there's also a Superbrands section where customers can get their hands on stylish names at a more reasonable price.

With a strong commitment to design, the company fosters emerging talent by combining with partners such as *Complex* magazine to co-curate, and celebrates fashion design moments with event series like Agender, which praised the groundbreaking androgynous fashion established by Comme des Garçons and Bodymap in the '80s and '90s. (££-£££)

See Chapter 4 for addresses and contact details.

Diverse

Established in 1987, Islington stalwart Diverse continues to attract and inspire generations of fashion-lovers with its beautiful contemporary men's and womenswear and accessories. Creative director Saskia Lamche has constantly innovated and introduced numerous iconic brands, while supporting the very best up-and-coming designers.

Spread over two floors, the boutique represents a comprehensive selection of established international designers, including Marc by Marc Jacobs, Diane von Furstenberg, Chloé, Emma Cook, Hussein Chalayan, Vanessa Bruno, Repetto and other big names. Diverse offers everything a modern chic wardrobe needs; ready-to-wear from Acne, Isabel Marant and Kenzo, denim from Hudson and Frame, and accessories from Céline and Opening Ceremony. Expensive, so keep an eye out for the sales.

Diverse, 294 Upper St, N1 2TU (020-7359 8877; http://diverseclothing.com; Angel tube; Mon-Sat 10.30am-6.30pm, Sun 11.30am-5.30pm; ££-£££).

Donna Ida

Opened in 2006 by Aussie Donna Ida Thornton – the Jean Queen of London – this Chelsea boutique (there's another in Elizabeth St, Belgravia) is *the* ultimate destination for premium designer jeans, featuring a bespoke denim wall, denim examination tables and vast luxurious fitting rooms. There's even a denim clinic (see website) where customers can book a one-on-one appointment with a style advisor to help find your perfect pair.

This is denim heaven with friendly and knowledgeable staff, stocking the world's best designer denim brands (Current/Elliott, Frame Design, J Brand, Paige – and their own IDA line) alongside complementary clothes and accessories such as blouses from Joie and Leon & Harper, T-shirts from Splendid and jumpers from Wildfox.

Donna Ida, 106 Draycott Ave, SW3 3AE (0207-225 3816; www.donnaida.com; S Kensington tube; Mon-Sat 10am-7pm, Sun noon-6pm; ££).

Emma Willis

Founded in 1987, with the Jermyn Street shop opening in 1999, Emma Willis is a traditional English shirt-maker – apart from the fact that she's a woman in a man's world. Emma uses luxurious Swiss and West Indian Sea Island cottons to make her top quality shirts, underwear, pyjamas, dressing gowns, socks, etc., using traditional methods of cutting and sewing.

Emma offers both ready-to-wear and bespoke shirts. You can visit the shop and have a fitting and paper shirt pattern made, which is kept at the factory in Gloucester so that you can order additional bespoke shirts online.

Emma Willis, 66 Jermyn St, SW1Y 6NY (020-7930 9980; www.emmawillis.com; Green Pk tube; Mon-Sat 10am-6pm, closed Sun; £££).

Feather & Stitch

Opened in 2009 by Fiona Sanderson – who cut her teeth travelling the globe as a buyer for a major high-street retailer – Feather & Stitch is a stylish Richmond boutique focusing on European (particularly Scandinavian) labels with a reputation for feminine, very wearable collections, such as Becksöndergaard, Filippa K, By Malene Birger, House of Dagmar, Des Petits Hauts and Samsøe & Samsøe.

Each season items are handpicked from mainly Scandinavian, French and other European designers with a focus on stylish everyday pieces such as well-cut jeans, luxurious knitwear, silk blouses and dresses, and beautiful shoes and accessories.

Feather & Stitch, 16 King St, Richmond, TW9 1ND (020-8332 2717; www.featherandstitch.com; Richmond tube/rail; Mon-Sat 10am-6pm, Sun 11am-5pm; ££-£££).

Feathers

Established in 1968 on Kensington High Street by Jean and William Burstein, Feathers is one of London's oldest independent luxury fashion boutiques – and a former employer of Manolo Blahnik. Located for the past 40 years in Knightsbridge, Feathers is run by 2nd and 3rd generation Bursteins (the family behind Browns), who constantly source fresh designers who compliment the boutique's niche, innovative spirit and clientele. The store is a haven for those seeking interesting contemporary designers, including Rick Owens, Ann Demeulemeester, Jil Sander, Junya Watanabe, Sacai and Haider Ackermann, to name just a few. A go-to boutique for great designer pieces.

Feathers Fashion, 42 Hans Cres, SW1X 0LZ (020-7589 5802; www.feathersfashion.com; Knightsbridge tube; Mon-Sat 10am-8pm, Sun noon-6pm; £££).

fleur b.

Former fashion buyer Fleur Bird opened her first boutique in 2008 and nowadays stocks a unique selection of contemporary, modern labels such as Carven, Filippa K, Paige Denim, Zoe Jordan, Goat, Mother Denim, American Vintage and Victoria Beckham Denim, alongside her own fleur b. collection launched in 2011.

Bird's own collection (now popularised by its diffusion in Anthropologie stores) is made in England and proudly champions British manufacturing. Her clothes are handcrafted from an array of beautiful fabrics such as luscious silks, silk wool mixes and butter-soft leather, making 'forever' pieces with a distinct London style. There's a second store at 8 Elystan Street in Chelsea (SW3).

fleur b., 21 Duke St, W1U 1DJ (020-7487 3915; www.fleurb.co.uk; Bond St tube; Mon-Sat 10.30am-6.30pm, Sun noon-6pm; ££-£££).

Folk

Founded in 2001 by Cathal McAteer (ex-Nicole Farhi, YMC) as a menswear brand, Folk is best known for the quiet, understated style on display in its three London stores. It added womenswear in 2012 and opened a shop for the girls a few steps away from its menswear store on Lamb's Conduit Street. Folk's clothes are high quality and best styled with extreme nonchalance – McAteer, a keen cyclist, insists on functionality. Expect high-quality natural fabrics, chic neutral colours, bold graphic prints and minimalist styling.

While predominantly an own- brand boutique, there's also a selection of complementary labels such as Sessun, Les Prairies de Paris and Tsumori Chisato. The frequent samples' sales are well worth checking out – oh, and for men, there's a barber's shop.

Folk, 49 (menswear) and 53 (womenswear) Lamb's Conduit St, WC1N 3NG (020-7404 6458; www.folkclothing.com; Russell Sq tube; Mon-Fri 11am-7pm, Sat 10am-6pm, Sun noon-5pm; ££-£££).

Glassworks

This ex-Covent Garden womenswear boutique made the leap east in 2014 and hasn't looked back since. Concessions for designers such as Helmut Lang, Sass and Bide and Jeffrey Campbell sit comfortably alongside newer, more affordable pieces that copy streetwear trends for fringing, ripped denim and whatever the latest thing is that girls have nicked from their boyfriend's wardrobe.

There are whole outfits to be built here, but shoppers on a flying visit should raid the accessories: chiffon socks, chunky sunglasses and pretty silver rings are just a few of the pieces of Shoreditch you can take home. There's also a branch in Dalston at 78 Stoke Newington Road.

Glassworks, 190 Shoreditch High St, E1 6HU (0845-410 0110; www.glassworks-studios.com; Shoreditch High St rail; Mon-Sat 11am-7pm, Sun noon-6pm; £-££).

Goat

Although its store opened only in 2014, Goat has been trading since 2001 when it was established by founder and designer Jane Lewis. It began life as a cashmere range for the fashion cognoscenti, but has since developed into a full ready-to-wear collection featuring dresses, tops, trousers and skirts, each piece individually tailored using the finest materials and finished to the highest standards.

The brand is synonymous with understated luxury – Victoria Beckham, Lana del Rey, Gwyneth Paltrow and the Duchess of Cambridge are among its celebrity clientele – and represents understated elegance for stylish, discerning (well-heeled) women.

Goat, 4 Conduit St, W1S 2DJ (020-7493 9323; www.goatfashion.com; Oxford Circus tube; Mon-Fri 9.30am-7pm, closed Sat-Sun; ££-£££).

The Goodhood Store

Established in 2007 by Kyle Stewart and Jo Sindle (ex-Levi's, Nike, Moschino), Goodhood is an award-winning lifestyle store and tastemaker offering pieces from over 200 different fashion, accessory, tech and homeware producers.

Firmly rooted in the East End, Goodhood draws from all over the world to represent good, innovative new designs in its two-floor location on Curtain Road. From streetwear like Dickie's to international designers such as Junya Watanabe, Goodhood covers a wide range of products but caters especially well for the young crowd (think skateboards, not Pinterest boards). They also favour curating their sections rather than letting trends dictate sales – a sure-fire sign that you're being offered the best there is.

The Goodhood Store, 151 Curtain Rd, EC2A 3QE (020-7729 3600; http://goodhoodstore.com; Old St tube/rail; Mon-Fri 10.30am-6.30pm, Sat 10.30am-7pm, Sun noon-6pm; ££).

Harrys of London

Founded in 2001, Kevin Martel took over as creative director of Harrys in 2005 and the gorgeous Mayfair flagship store opened in 2008, offering a stylish if pricey fusion of footwear, marrying traditional cobbling with the latest technology. Their stated mission is 'to create innovative footwear and accessories defined by exceptional quality, design and technology, balancing respect for tradition while embracing the future'.

Known for its innovative and beautifully crafted shoes designed to merge easy wearability with the versatility of a rubber sole, Harrys has a loyal following of clients who are drawn to its quality and timeless design. Not cheap but a real treat for feet.

Harrys of London, 59 South Audley St, W1K 2QN (020-7409 7988; www.harrysoflondon.com; Green/Hyde Pk tube; Mon-Wed, Fri-Sat 10am-6pm, Thu 10am-7pm, closed Sun; £££).

Heidi Klein

Launched in 2002 by Heidi Gosman and Penny Klein, Heidi Klein was the UK's first one-stop holiday shop with a fabulous selection of exquisitely-cut swimwear, cover-ups and accessories. The Notting Hill boutique (there's another in SW1) is evocative of a Caribbean retreat in whitewashed wood adorned with palm leaves, bleached coral and driftwood, complete with the delicate scent of coconut. There's also an on-site beauty salon offering waxing, tanning, facials and manicures.

Heidi Klein's chic and elegant designs have earned it a celebrity following from the likes of Kate Moss, Sienna Miller and Jennifer Aniston, as well as kudos from the fashion press and a loyal customer base.

Heidi Klein, 174 Westbourne Grove, W11 2RW (020-7243 5665; www.heidiklein.com; Notting Hill Gate tube; Mon-Sat 10am-6pm, Sun noon-5pm; ££-£££).

Hostem

Opened in 2010, menswear (now also offering womenswear) boutique Hostem in Shoreditch was conceived by James Brown (no, not that one!) and launched with a fantastic collection of distinguished luxury labels from around the globe. Designed by husband and wife team James Russell and Hannah Plumb (aka James Plumb) – low lit and forged from reclaimed (often antique) materials with an abundance of distressed wood – the boutique feels more like a gallery space than a shop.

Hostem has become a cult destination with an avant-garde approach to fashion, where you'll find designers such as Yang Li, Dries Van Noten, Achilles Ion Gabriel, Simone Rocha, Yohji Yamamoto, Alice Waese and Casely-Hayford.

Hostem, 28 Old Nichol St, E2 7HR (020-7739 9733; www.hostem.co.uk; Shoreditch High St rail; Mon-Sat 11am-7pm, Sun noon-6pm; ££-£££).

Hub

A popular boutique with a loyal following, Hub (owned by Louise Power and Georgie Cook) has both men's and women's boutiques on Stoke Newington Church Street. It offers a good selection of mid-range staples from Custom Made, Wood Wood, Libertine-Libertine, Sessun, Great Plains, Vagabond and Beth Graham (designed by Power), alongside bags from Ally Capellino and Sandqvist plus other accessories.

Over the road at no 88, Hub Men stocks many of the same labels as the women's boutique, as well as knits by John Smedley and a selection of items from Farah, Folk, YMC, Universal Works, Bethnals, Saucony and more.

Hub, 49 (Womenswear) and 88 (Menswear) Stoke Newington Church St, London N16 0AR/0AP (020-7524 4494, menswear 020-7275 8160; http:// hubshop.co.uk; Stoke Newington rail; Mon-Sat 10.30am-6pm, Sun 11am-5pm; £-££).

Iris

Launched by Annie Pollet and Sarah Claassen in 2004 in Queen's Park, Iris has since expanded to four boutiques: Queen's Park, Chiswick, Amersham and Northcote Road, featured here. Annie had an extensive fashion background working for Calvin Klein, Nicole Farhi and Earl Jeans, while Sarah was the head of jewellery production and sales at luxury jeweller David Morris (see page 183).

The ultimate yummy mummy's neighbourhood boutique, Iris sells desirable, stylish womenswear, children's clothes, accessories and gifts. Labels stocked include Alöe, American Vintage, BA&SH, Chinti & Parker, Duffy, Hudson, Isabel Marant Etoile, Sessun, Vanessa Bruno Athé and many more.

Iris, 97 Northcote Rd, SW11 6PL (020-7924 1836; www.irisfashion.co.uk; Clapham S tube; Mon-Sat 10am-6pm, Sun 11am-5pm; ££).

James Lock & Co

The oldest hat shop in the world (also the world's oldest family-owned business), James Lock & Co was founded in 1676 by Robert Davis. Over the centuries Lock & Co

have supplied headwear to the cream of London society, including Winston Churchill, Charlie Chaplin, the Duke of Wellington and Admiral Lord Nelson, along with the British royal family (it currently holds royal warrants for the Prince of Wales and the Duke of Edinburgh).

Nowadays the ranges and selection of headwear is ever changing and, while still providing traditional and functional styles, Lock's manages to keep pace with fashion and current trends (for both ladies and gentlemen).

James Lock & Co, 6 St James's St, SW1A 1EF (020-7930 8874; www.lockhatters.co.uk; Green Pk tube; Mon-Fri 9am-5.30pm, Sat 9.30am-5pm, closed Sun; ££-£££).

KJ's Laundry

The lovechild of Jane Ellis and Kate Allden, KJ's Laundry opened in 2006 on Marylebone Lane. It's dedicated to seeking out the season's most stylish designer clothes and accessories from the most interesting and wearable labels – including both established and less well-known designers – from around the globe. The wide-ranging stock includes celebrated names such as Vanessa

Bruno Athé, Humanoid, IRO, Filippa K and IRO alongside cult favourites like Samantha Sung, Sessun, Ilaria Nistri Roque, Studio Nicholson and BA&SH, plus new finds such as Dagmar, Rabens Saloner, Thakoon Addition, Currer Bell and Sandqvist bags.

The beautiful low-key boutique is a pleasure to visit, with helpful and friendly staff.

KJ's Laundry, 74 Marylebone Ln, W1U 2PW (020-7486 7855; www.kjslaundry.com; Bond St tube; Mon-Sat 10am-7pm, Sun 11am-5pm; ££).

Kokon To Zai

Established in Greek St, Soho in 1996, fashion outlet Kokon To Zai (it means 'east meets west' in Japanese) is the brainchild of Macedonian design duo Marjan Pejoski and Sasha Bezovski. The Golborne Road store (there's a third shop in Paris) features original mosaic tiled floors – it was previously a butcher's shop – which are the backdrop to a cornucopia of skulls in bell jars, butterflies, ornamental umbrellas, sculpture, antique pieces and taxidermy, all of which help give Koton To Zai its quirky cutting edge.

KTZ specialises in avant-garde weird and wonderful fashion for both men and women – heavily influenced by punk, Goth and the Orient – wacky interior design pieces and a funky line in jewellery.

Kokon To Zai, 86 Golborne Rd, W10 5PS (020-8960 3736; www.kokontozai.co.uk; Westbourne Pk tube; Mon-Sat 10am-6pm, closed Sun; ££-£££).

LN-CC

An ultra cool Dalston lifestyle store for both men and women, LN-CC (short for Late Night Chameleon Café) is an innovative retail concept, with a physical store – housed within an art-based installation – which you can visit by making an appointment or (if you're lucky) ringing the doorbell, as well as an online store. It redefines the perception of modern retailing in a personally curated, if slightly over-exclusive, way.

LN-CC offers menswear, womenswear, accessories, music and books, and in its physical guise includes a library, record store, gallery, and a club space and bar. Expect to find emerging talents alongside more established names such as Lanvin, Saint Laurent, Stella McCartney, Calvin Klein, Balenciaga, Haider Ackermann and Maxwell Snow.

LN-CC, The Basement, 18-24 Shacklewell Ln, E8 2EZ (020-7275 7265; www.ln-cc.com; Dalston Kingsland rail; Mon-Sat 10am-6pm, Sun 11am-4pm; £££).

Lowie

Fair, but by no means square, Lowie was founded by designer Bronwyn Lowenthal in 2002 as a vintage-inspired fashion label with a commitment to producing its collections as ethically as possible; Lowenthal's philosophy is to create beautifully designed clothes with minimal environmental impact, by using workers in small factories that pay a fair wage. Sought-after pieces include classic tea dresses and cashmere berets from the softest wools and pure cottons, lovingly handmade and often designed in-house.

It's also a great place to check out affordable ethical costume jewellery and gifts by London designers and makers.

Lowie, 115 Dulwich Rd, SE24 0NG (020-7733 0040; http://ilovelowie.com; Herne Hill rail; Tue 11am-5pm, Wed-Sat 10am-6pm, Sun 11am-5pm, closed Mon; ££).

Luna & Curious

Established in 2006, Luna & Curious is an inspired collective with an exquisite lifestyle boutique in Shoreditch's historic Boundary Estate. Owned and run by a group of designers (Polly George, Rheanna Lingham and Kaoru Parry), the shop offers a cornucopia of clothing (womenswear and childrenswear), jewellery, ceramics, etc., representing value, craftsmanship and beauty. The trio are passionate about great British design and offer display space to emerging designers, while themed events create a fresh and inspiring vibe.

Prices are surprisingly reasonable for products so lovingly crafted. The collective also accepts bespoke commissions.

Luna & Curious, 24-26 Calvert Ave, E2 7JP (020-3222 0034; http://lunaandcurious.com; Shoreditch High St tube; Mon-Sat 11am-6pm, Sun 11am-5pm; £-££).

Machine-A

An independent concept store for men and women, Machine-A (in partnership with SHOWstudio) is the brainchild of Stavros Karelis, focusing on exceptional British and international contemporary fashion design. A showcase for London fashion's energy and optimism, it sells many interesting and current collections from established brands alongside exclusive pieces from an irreverent breed of young undiscovered talent.

The store stocks many of the capital's edgiest and hippest labels, including Ambush, Cottweiler, Hyein SEO, Liam Hodges, Nasir Mazhar, Raf Simons, Sibling and Tigran Avetisyan. Machine-A is one of London's must-visit independent boutiques for those who know their fashion – different, exclusive and expensive.

Machine-A, 13 Brewer St, W1F 0RH (020-7734 4334; www.machine-a.com; Piccadilly Circus tube; Mon-Wed 11am-7pm, Thu-Sat 11am-8pm, Sun noon-6pm; £££).

Matches Fashion

Tom and Ruth Chapman opened their first Matches boutique in Wimbledon Village in 1987 and were the first retailer in the UK to stock Prada. Now with five London stores (Marylebone, two in Notting Hill, Richmond and Wimbledon) and a massive online business, Matches is one of London's most successful luxury fashion boutiques.

Its Notting Hill store showcases an edit of over 400 established and emerging menswear and womenswear designers, from Saint Laurent, Balenciaga, Burberry Prorsum, Christian Louboutin, Chloé and Isabel Marant, to Alexander McQueen, Gucci, Dolce & Gabbana, Diane von Furstenberg, Lanvin, Stella McCartney and Max Mara. Matches also offers free fashion advice through its online service MyStylist.

Matches Fashion, 60-64 Ledbury Rd, W11 2AJ (020-7221 0255; www.matchesfashion.com; Notting Hill Gate tube; Mon-Wed 10am-6pm, Thu-Sat 10am-7pm, Sun noon-6pm; ££-£££).

The Mercantile London

A womenswear boutique (owned by Debra and Thomas McCann) in Spitalfields, East London, Mercantile has a laid-back, welcoming vibe, showcasing a beautifully curated selection of labels from across the world, both established and new, large and small, affordable and designer, including new cult womenswear brand 2nd Day and Bill Skinner's nature-inspired jewellery.

The boutique offers an eclectic mix of everything from tailoring to outerwear, a vast array of denim, cute dresses and easy tops, alongside attractive jewellery, accessories, footwear, apothecary and gifts. The clothes appeal to women with the confidence to mix designer with vintage, new and old; and the heavy footfall and constant turnover means there's always something fresh and new in store.

The Mercantile, 17 Spitalfields Arts Market, Lamb St, E1 6EA (020-7377 8926; www.themercantilelondon.com; Shoreditch High St rail; Mon-Sat 10am-7pm, Sun 10am-6pm; £-££).

Merchant Archive

Begun in 2007 when Sophie Merchant began sourcing and selling vintage clothes to designers for inspiration, Merchant Archive soon progressed via a small retail space in Queen's Park to its current beautiful flagship store on Kensington Park Road in Notting Hill. The boutique offers an in-house collection of ready-to-wear, homeware and accessories, as well as luxury vintage clothing, jewellery and accessories, antique furniture, objets d'art, contemporary designer eyewear and footwear.

Sophie's discerning eye is evident in the expertly-edited selection of beautiful one-off antique pieces, with vintage numbers from Lanvin, jumpsuits from the '20s, antique velvet jackets, a good choice of elegant dresses and some lovely jewellery.

Merchant Archive, 19 Kensington Park Rd, W11 2EU (020-7229 9006; www.merchantarchive.com; Ladbroke Grove tube; Mon-Sat 10am-6pm, Sun noon-5pm; ££-£££).

Mouki Mou

Maria Lemos directs the influential fashion showroom that launched the careers of leading designers such as Peter Pilotto, Rachel Comey and Meadham Kirchhoff. She also runs a small lifestyle boutique, Off the Beaten Track, that showcases the best clothing and homeware she comes across at the cutting edge of the British fashion design industry.

Much of the tiny collection is artisanal – the hand-knotted scarves from a women's cooperative in Sardinia, or the hand-sewn leather loafers whose colours change with the seasons – but alongside the short runs of handmade accessories and homeware you'll find designer pieces by RainbowWave names such as Tim Coppens. The store's also good for mid-price gifts, such as simple geometric jewellery from a New York designer or Danish ceramics.

Mouki Mou, 29 Chiltern St, W1U 7PL (020-7224 4010; www.moukimou.com; Baker St tube; Mon-Fri 11am-7pm, Sat 10am-6pm, Sun noon-5pm; ££-£££).

Oliver Spencer

After starting out with a market stall at Portobello Market, self-taught tailor Oliver Spencer established his brand in 2002, having spent the previous decade creating and expanding formalwear brand Favourbrook. Oli's vision was to create a range of clothing with all the quality and craft of premium tailoring, but with a relaxed modern style.

From a single store on Lamb's Conduit Street (now two stores – no 62 stocks clothes, while 58 offers accessories and shoes), Oliver Spencer now has five stores (four in London), is stocked by the world's top department stores and has an international online business.

Oliver Spencer, 58 & 62 Lamb's Conduit St, WC1N 3LW (clothes 020-7269 6444, accessories 020-7831 3483; http://oliverspencer.co.uk; Russell Sq tube; Mon-Sat 11am-7pm, Sun noon-5pm; ££-£££).

Oliver Sweeney

Founded in 1989, Oliver Sweeney (now co-owned by MD and cobbler-in-chief Tim Cooper) is a luxury lifestyle brand for men, one that's synonymous with quality and style. It specialises in the design and manufacture of classic men's shoes (namely brogues, boots and loafers) but also offers menswear and accessories.

The brand prides itself on its handcrafted processes, finest English and Italian leather, and the originality of its designs, which ensures that Oliver Sweeney shoes remain a perennial favourite among hipsters and celebrities alike. You can even have your shoes tattooed, and the flagship Henrietta Street store offers a polishing service.

Oliver Sweeney, 10 Henrietta St, WC2E 8PS (020-7240 4549; www.oliversweeney.com; Covent Gdn tube; Mon-Wed 10am-7pm, Thu 10am-8pm, Fri-Sat 10am-7pm, Sun noon-6pm; ££).

Other Shop

Established in 2012 by Matthew Murphy and Kirk Beattie (formerly of b Store), Other Shop is an independent boutique for hard-to-find labels and new talent. Beloved of fashion insiders, independence is key here; it's the sole stockist for some designers and acts as a showcase and hothouse for up-and-coming newcomers.

Two-thirds of the pieces are made by Other's own label, while the remainder is made up of guest names such as Scandi brands FWSS and Our Legacy, Novesta (handmade shoes), and cult ready-to-wear brand Lemaire. You can also give your fashion-weary eyes a rest by enjoying the store's selection of fashion magazines and the occasional in-store exhibitions. A destination store for a host of reasons.

Other Shop, 21 Kingly St, W1B 5QA (020-7734 6846; www.other-shop.com; Oxford Circus tube; Mon-Sat 10.30am-6.30pm, Sun noon-5pm; ££).

Oxygen Boutique

Light, spacious, and central, no wonder Oxygen has become one of London's fashion stalwarts. After many years making clothes for chains such as Zara, mother-daughter duo Helen and Joanna Nicola opened their own venue in Fitzrovia: a fashion store offering a unique mix of hot new, up-and-coming designers alongside cult brands.

The boutique stocks some of the most coveted labels from New York and beyond, including Alexis, Clover Canyon, Mara Hoffman, Giuseppe Zanotti, Alice+Olivia, For Love and Lemons, Frame Denim and Carven, as well as in-house designs from brand Related, and a range of shoes, accessories, jewellery, fashion and art books by Taschen. For fans of US brands, there's nowhere like it.

Oxygen Boutique, 51 Eastcastle St, W1W 8EB (020-7636 6001; www.oxygenboutique.com; Oxford Circus tube; Mon-Fri 11am-6.30pm, closed Sat-Sun; ££-£££).

Pokit

Founded in 1999 by Bayode Oduwole and Claire Pringle, Pokit are 'contemporary outfitters of fine modern tailoring' for both men and women, plus handsome leather bags and canvas holdalls. Pokit are proud of the fact that 99 per cent of their products are made in England by master craftsmen and women to the most exacting standards and from the very best materials.

The handsome London store is filled with immaculate leather goods including shoes, wallets, belts and bags, which play a supporting role to the custom-made tailored suits, made from robust, rugged fabrics – tweed, white linen, navy cotton, corduroy – sourced from British and Irish mills. Savile Row quality – and prices to match.

Pokit, 17 St Anne's Ct, W1W 0BQ (020-7434 2875; www.pokit.co.uk; Oxford Circus tube; Mon-Fri 11am-7pm, Sat noon-5pm, closed Sun; £££).

Poste Mistress

The high profile (younger, cuter and more exclusive) sister of popular high-street chain Office Shoes, Poste Mistress in Covent Garden offers reasonably priced quality women's footwear in a fun retro boudoir setting (there's also a Poste boutique for men at 10 South Molton Street).

As well as its own-brand range, PM includes a range of designer favourites including Acne, Chie Mihara, Dries Van Noten, Eley Kishimoto, Jil Sander, Lulu Guinness, Miu Miu, Opening Ceremony, Stella McCartney and Vivienne Westwood. There's also a good range of casual footwear from the likes of Converse and Melissa.

Poste Mistress, 61-63 Monmouth St, WC2H 9EP (020-7379 4040; www.office.co.uk/brand/poste_mistress; Covent Gdn tube; Mon-Wed, Fri-Sat 10am-7pm, Thu 10am-8pm, Sun 11.30-6pm; £-££).

Present

Created by Eddie Prendergast and Steve Davies – founders of men's mega-brand Duffer of St George – Present is an Aladdin's cave offering virtually anything and everything for the man about town. Present stocks an eclectic collection of modern, dandyish pieces from far and wide, including labels such as Aquascutum, Pendleton, Maharishi, Archie Foal, Haversack, Alltimers, Hartford, Esemplare and many more, plus its own range of shoes in collaboration with Trickers and the owners' collection of knitwear and T-shirts.

There's also a range of art books, magazines, notebooks, wallets, watches, gadgetry, gifts and accessories – and a coffee machine.

Present, 140 Shoreditch High St, E1 6JE (020-7033 0500; www.present-london.com; Shoreditch High St rail/Old St tube; Mon-Fri 10.30am-7pm, Sat 11am-6.30pm, Sun 11am-5pm; ££).

Richard James

Founded in 1992, Richard James is the new kid on the block when it comes to bespoke Savile Row tailors – the so-called 'new bespoke movement' – although he quickly established a reputation as a premier luxury brand. The company was awarded the coveted British Fashion Council's Menswear Designer of the Year (2001) and Bespoke Designer of the Year (2008).

RJ's philosophy is to produce everyday clothing of unsurpassable quality, but to push the boundaries through design, colour and cut. It produces updated classics – contemporary design with an exacting attention to detail – and works closely with woollen mills and artisans in Britain and Italy to design and produce its exclusive fabrics and handmade accessories.

Richard James, 29 Savile Row, W1S 2EY (020-7434 0605; www.richardjames.co.uk; Piccadilly Circus tube; Mon-Wed, Fri-Sat 10am-6pm, Thu 10am-7pm, closed Sun; £££).

The Shop at Bluebird

One of London's most acclaimed concept stores, the vast 10,000ft^2 Shop at Bluebird offers a wealth of high-end designers alongside niche labels and emerging fashion talent, interspersed with *objets*, ephemera, books, music and cult beauty brands. Curated by John and Belle Robinson – the creative force behind Jigsaw – Bluebird's team strives to create an eclectic experience that's both laid back and luxurious, where you can browse and buy the perfect outfit with the help of the store's personal shoppers; there's also a great beauty bar.

It's a stimulating and inspiring taste of vibrant '60s Chelsea, and when you've finished splurging, you can treat yourself to lunch at the Bluebird café next door.

The Shop at Bluebird, 350 King's Rd, SW3 5UU (020-7351 3873; www.theshopatbluebird.com; Sloane Sq tube; Mon-Sat 10am-7pm, Sun noon-6pm; ££-£££).

Sixty6

Originally opened in 1997 at 66 Marylebone Street (hence the name), Sixty6 is a chic womenswear boutique owned by Jane Collins, which recently reopened in larger premises in Bulstrode Street. It stocks a host of leading designers including Osman, Sara C, Just In Case, Essentiel, 360 Sweater, Geoffrey's of London, Talbot Runhof, Rebecca Taylor, Jean-Pierre Braganza, Georgia Hardinge, and cashmere from Magaschoni and Madeleine Thompson. There are also lovely accessories and beautiful contemporary and vintage costume jewellery.

Sixty6 offers an eclectic selection of clothes for all occasions and appeals to those with a sense of individuality who want something a little different.

Sixty6, 17 Bulstrode St, W1U 2JH (020-7935 3705; www.sixty-6.com; Bond St tube; Mon-Sat 10.30am-6.30pm, Sun 1-5pm; ££-£££).

Son of a Stag

One of London's best men's jeans and streetwear specialists, Son of a Stag (also known as JFK Clothing) was started in 2003 by Danish knitwear designer Torben Hjorth – the surname means stag in Danish.

SoaS carry the best and largest choice of Japanese and American denim (and footwear) brands such as Big John, Copper King, Edwin, Endrime, Full Count, Heller's Cafe, Kojima Genes, Lee Archives, Momotaro, Omnigod, Orgueil, Pherrow's, Raleigh, Samurai, Spellbound, Studio D'artisan, TCB, Tellason and Warehouse & Co. It's also the only store in the UK to offer on-the-spot hemming alterations with an original Union Special chainstitch machine.

Son of a Stag, 91 Brick Ln, E1 6QL (020-7247 3333; www.sonofastag.com; Liverpool St tube/ rail; Mon-Wed, Fri-Sat 10.30am-7pm, Thu 10.30am-8pm, Sun 11am-6pm; ££-£££).

Square One

A third-generation luxury fashion boutique run by Beverley and Gary Vanger, Square One has separate men's and women's stores in upmarket St John's Wood High Street, stocking a wide variety of everything from jeans and jackets to knitwear, footwear and dresses to accessories and more. Clothes are sourced from around the world and range from beautifully crafted heritage pieces to cutting-edge contemporary items, carefully handpicked from the best and most fashionable labels and the latest trends.

In recent years Square One has become something of a denim powerhouse, with complementary trendsetting separates.

Square One, 43 & 51A St John's Wood High St, NW8 7NJ (020-7586 8658/8605; http:// squareonelondon.com; St John's Wood tube; Mon-Sat 10am-6pm, Sun 11.30am-5.30pm; £££).

Topshop, Oxford Street

For both value for money and choice, nothing can match Topshop's flagship Oxford Circus megastore, which offers five floors of affordable men's and women's fashion, new designers, catwalk inspired looks, accessories and more from the UK's biggest fashion chain. From iconic labels to up-and-coming names, the store stocks a wide array of brands, including Adidas, Calvin Klein, Ellesse, Kappa, Hype, Rains and Religion (plus own brands Boutique and Unique), to name just a few.

The store was recently relaunched with a host of innovative new features, including a personal shopping lounge, barber shop and hairdressing, tattooing, wig-fitting, plus a huge variety of concessions. There's a basement café for pit stops, too.

Topshop, 214 Oxford St, W1W 8LG (0844-848 7487; www.topshop.com; Oxford Circus tube; Mon-Sat 9.30am-9pm, Sun noon-6pm; £-££).

Trilogy

Founded in 2006 by Lesley Torson, Trilogy is one of London's best women's denim specialists and the place to head for the perfect pair of jeans. Now with five London stores (Chelsea, Hampstead, Kensington, Marylebone and Wimbledon), it's grown to become a destination store for top-to-toe styling, rather than simply a denim specialist.

The Chelsea store stocks a massive choice of denim (over two floors) from the likes of Adriano Goldschmied (AG), Current Elliott, Frame, J Brand, James, L'Agence, MIH and Paige, plus some of the hottest contemporary brands around including Tucker, Vince and Velvet, as well as great everyday basics from American Vintage and Splendid. Sheer jeanius!

Trilogy, 31 Duke of York Sq, SW3 4LY (020-7730 6515; www.trilogystores.co.uk; Sloane Sq tube; Mon-Sat 10am-6.30pm, Sun noon-6pm; ££-£££).

Trunk

Launched in 2010, Trunk now has two stores on hip Chiltern Street, Trunk Clothiers at no. 8 and Trunk Labs at no. 34. Trunk Clothiers is a cosy neighbourhood shop featuring collections of the best menswear and accessories from Britain, Italy, Japan, Sweden, the US and beyond, while Trunk Labs is a 'lifestyle' shop stocking a selection of the finest clothing, accessories, luggage, bags, shoes, belts and small leather goods, along with grooming products, stationery, eyewear, homeware, gifts and even furniture.

Trunk brings together a lovingly curated range, setting a new standard for gentlemen seeking modern classics and accessories of the highest quality.

Trunk, 8 & 34 Chiltern St, W1U 7PU/7QH (020-7486 2357; www.trunkclothiers.com; Baker St tube; Mon-Fri 11am-7pm, Sat 11am-6pm, Sun noon-5pm; ££-£££).

Uniqlo

With some 850 stores in Japan and another 800 worldwide, Japanese superstore Uniqlo is hardly your typical independent London boutique. It opened its first store outside Japan in London in 2001, which was followed in 2007 by its global flagship (and largest) store on Oxford Street. It now boasts ten stores in and around London.

Uniqlo caters to the environmentally-conscious man and woman who wants good quality, long-lasting clothing at an affordable price, and is best known for its huge range of inexpensive basics and iconic colourful puffer jackets. When it comes to value for money this Japanese powerhouse is hard to beat. There's also a same-day alterations service.

Uniqlo, 311 Oxford St, W1C 2HP (020-7016 1500; www.uniqlo.com/uk; Bond St/Oxford Circus tube; Mon-Sat 10am-9pm, Sun noon-6pm; £).

Universal Works

Universal Works began life in 2008 with David Keyte (co-founder, director, designer – previously with Paul Smith and Maharishi, among others) working from his kitchen table. Keyte now has two stores in London and sells worldwide from Los Angeles to Seoul. UW's simple, classically-cut clothes are timeless, based on fit and good design, inspired by traditional British workwear, and produced in small batches by skilled workers in bijou factories.

Check out Keyte's designs at his ultra-cool Lamb's Conduit store (or visit the other shop on Berwick Street, W1).

Universal Works, 37 Lamb's Conduit St, WC1N 3NG (020-3632 2115; www.universalworks.co.uk; Russell Sq tube; Mon-Sat 11am-7pm, Sun 11am-5pm; ££).

The Vintage Showroom

Founded in 2007 to house the expanding archive of vintage clothes and accessories collected by co-founders Douglas Gunn and Roy Luckett, The Vintage Showroom is now one of London's best resources for vintage menswear. The boutique in Seven Dials (Covent Garden) was opened in 2009, occupying the former iconic hardware store of FW Collins & Sons (est. 1835).

The expertly curated selection of vintage menswear ranges from the mid-20th century to the '80s, specialising in international work, military and sportswear, classic English tailoring and country wear, including a wide choice of designer coats from Barbour to Belstaff.

The Vintage Showroom, 14 Earlham St, WC2H 9LN (020-7836 3964; www.thevintageshowroom. com; Covent Gdn tube; Tue-Sat 11am-7.30pm, Sun noon-6pm; £-££).

Wolf & Badger

Opened in Notting Hill in 2009 by brothers Henry and George Graham, Wolf & Badger quickly established itself as a leading retailer of independent fashion, jewellery and accessories from the UK and beyond. The boutique's slick interior and enticing window displays showcase

a beguiling collection from emerging designers who lease space in the store. W&B specialises in costume jewellery: iconic London designs such as Harry Rocks' constellation pendants and Tessa Metcalfe's eagle claw rings make a great souvenir for any *Vogue* subscriber's trip to London.

W&B is a powerhouse that discovers and supports small independent designers from around the world. There's a second shop in Dover Street, W1.

Wolf & Badger, 46 Ledbury Rd, W11 2AB (020-7229 5698; www.wolfandbadger.com; Notting Hill Gate tube; Mon-Sat 10am-6.30pm, Sun 11am-5pm; £-££).

YMC (You Must Create)

Formed in 1995 by Fraser Moss and Jimmy Collins, YMC (You Must Create) – inspired by industrial designer Raymond Loewy, who, when asked how he saw the future of design, replied 'You must create your own style' – has spent 20 years developing and evolving its unique functional men's and womenswear, which eschews trends in favour of understated and wearable style with a twist. One example of YMC's classic constructions is its cotton rain mac, where minimalist details such as drawstring ties and tortoiseshell buttons create chic clean lines and demonstrate the longstanding appeal of YMC designs.

The brand's take on well-designed and quality clothes for an active urban customer has stuck a chord with the fashion media, buyers and punters alike. Also in Poland St, W1.

YMC, 23 Hanbury St, E1 6QR (020-3432 3010; www.youmustcreate.com; Shoreditch High St rail; Mon-Sat 11am-7pm, Sun noon-6pm; ££).

Verde & Company

6.
Food & Drink

When it comes to food shopping, Londoners have never had it so good. The city has been reborn as a foodie paradise with an abundance of artisan food shops, delicatessens, food halls, ethnic stores and a huge number of markets (see **Chapter 9**). From this enormous edible bounty we have selected some of the very best places to buy artisan food, be it the best of British fare – handmade cheese, bread and charcuterie – or exotic produce from all corners of the globe, such as handpicked spices, single-estate coffee and extra-virgin oils.

We couldn't overlook the food halls of the major department stores, their counters heaving with caviar, truffles, foie gras and more; however, they cater for shoppers with deep pockets and are, for most of us, somewhere to buy a treat rather than do the weekly shop. This chapter focuses on the smaller independent stores, the butchers, bakers and cupcake makers who are dedicated to offering great choice, in-depth knowledge and artisan quality at affordable prices; all committed to the quality and provenance of their produce.

From Jamaican coffee to the finest wines, fresh-off-the-boat fish to meticulously-aged cheese, and jamón ibérico to Dorset knobs – you can eat and drink it all in London.

Algerian Coffee Stores

The name is a bit of a misnomer, as the Algerian Coffee Stores (plural, although there's only one) specialises in coffee **and** tea. Established in 1887, this aromatic little shop still boasts many of its original features, including its rustic wooden shelving, counter and display case. Based in Soho, it stocks over 80 blends of coffee and 120 kinds of tea from around the world. The huge range of coffees includes a large number of house blends alongside single-origin, organic and Fairtrade beans, as well as flavoured and spiced beans (such as Lebanese with cardamom) and rarities such as Indonesian Kopi Luwak, made from beans that have been eaten and passed undigested by civet cats!

Algerian Coffee Stores also sell drinking chocolate and cocoa, a range of confectionery (truffles, Turkish delight, etc.) and spices, plus domestic coffee machines, grinders, milk frothers, tea strainers and more. You can buy supplies online too. It's also a great-value place to drink coffee: an espresso is just £1 and a cappuccino or latte £1.20 (take-away or standing only), with an extra shot free.

Algerian Coffee Stores, 52 Old Compton St, W1D 4PB (020-7437 2480; www.algcoffee.co.uk; Leicester Sq tube; Mon-Wed 9am-7pm, Thu-Fri 9am-9pm, Sat 9am-8pm, closed Sun).

Berry Bros & Rudd

The oldest wine and spirit merchant in Britain (and probably the world), Berry Bros & Rudd has traded from the same premises since 1698. Berry Bros first supplied wine to the Royal Family during the reign of George III and continues to do so today (it currently holds two royal warrants). The shop resembles a time capsule, having changed little in over 300 years, while its vast cellars – running under the courtyard as far as Pall Mall – contain over 200,000 bottles. Today members of the Berry and Rudd families continue to own and manage the family-run wine merchant.

Berry Bros & Rudd won three awards at the 2014 International Wine Challenge, including Specialist Merchant of the Year En Primeur, Large Independent of the Year and the top award, Wine Merchant of the Year. Not only is Berry Bros London's premier wine dealer, it's also a leading provider of wine masterclasses, and was Wine Educator of the Year at the 2012 International Wine Challenge. So, whether you wish to buy wine for pleasure or investment, expand your wine know-how or become an expert, Berry Bros is your one-stop shop.

Berry Bros & Rudd, 3 St James's St, SW1A 1EG (0800-280 2440/020-7022 8973; www.bbr.com; Green Pk tube; Mon-Fri 10am-9pm, Sat 10am-5pm, closed Sun).

Biscuiteers

Founded in 2007 by passionate biscuit makers Harriet Hastings and Stevie Congdon, Biscuiteers' USP is, of course, biscuits – but not any old biscuits. They're famous for their personalised, handmade luxury biscuits, which they sell at their delightful 'biscuit boutique & icing café' in Notting Hill. Other tasty offerings include cakes, traditional sweets, hand-iced cupcakes, macarons and customised chocolates, which can be decorated with flowers and letters to spell out a message. The shop also offers icing classes, where you too can learn how to become a biscuiteer.

Biscuiteers, 194 Kensington Park Rd, W11 2ES (020-7727 8096; www.biscuiteers.com; Ladbroke Grove tube; Mon-Sat 10am-6pm, Sun 11am-5pm).

Bottle Apostle

Bottle Apostle is a new kid on the block, with just five outlets: Hackney, Clapham, Crouch End, Stratford East Village and Primrose Hill. Their first shop (Hackney) opened only in 2009 but they quickly gained an enviable reputation for their wines and expertise and also for their approachability, and it was judged Britain's Best Small Wine Shop in 2011 by *The Daily Telegraph*. All stores have Enomatic sampling machines, which allow you to try before you buy, and host regular informal wine-tasting events. They also stock ciders and craft beers from London's top artisan breweries.

Bottle Apostle, 95 Lauriston Rd, E9 7HJ (020-8985 1549; www.bottleapostle.com; Cambridge Heath/London Fields rail; Mon-Fri noon-9pm, Sat 10am-8pm, Sun 10am-6pm).

Bumblebee

Bumblebee (they keep bees in the garden behind the shop) has been a north London institution for 25 years, during which it has spread along Brecknock Road where it now occupies three shops. It comprises a grocer (the original store), greengrocer and bakery, and offers a comprehensive range of vegetarian and organic foods, household goods and natural remedies.

Bumblebee's ethos is to offer quality foods at reasonable prices, and it stocks many locally produced products. Services include a vegetable box scheme – free local delivery of seasonal fruit and veg – and hot takeaway food at lunchtime.

Bumblebee, 33 Brecknock Rd, N7 0BT (020-7284 1314/020-7607 1936; www.bumblebee.london; Caledonian Rd tube; Mon-Sat 9am-6.30pm, closed Sun).

Damas Gate

Founded in 1989, Damas Gate is one of the oldest Middle-Eastern food wholesalers in the UK, as well as being the first to sell halal products. DG's bustling supermarket on Uxbridge Road typifies their dedication to the quality and provenance of their food, and their understanding of customers' needs. It's an Aladdin's cave of edible goodies with aisles overflowing with olives, nuts and dates, pickles and pulses, herbs and spices, and flatbreads and pastries; fridges full of sheep's cheese and yogurt, ready-to-eat falafels and kebabs, mounds of fresh fruit and veg, plus a halal butcher's counter.

Damas Gate, 81-85 Uxbridge Rd, W12 8NR (020-8743 5116; www.damasgate.uk.com; Shepherd's Bush Mkt tube; daily 9am-10pm).

Daylesford Organic

A pioneer of organic farming, Daylesford have been established for over 30 years and are one of the most respected food producers in the UK. All their produce travels directly from farm to fork: meat and poultry from their pastures, fruit and vegetables from their market garden, bread from their bakery, and cheese, milk and yoghurt from their creamery. Daylesford grow over 300 varieties of organic fruit, vegetables, salad leaves and herbs on their 20-acre farm in Gloucestershire, including many unusual and heritage varieties. They also offer a range of award-winning ready-to-cook meals, soups, jams and chutneys, made from their own produce whenever possible.

Pimlico was Daylesford's first London base and it now hosts a farm shop and organic café. This large, well-designed shop, with its clean white spaces and grey marble, offers three floors of top quality organic food to eat in or take home. What's more it's located near Mozart Square, a pretty pedestrianised space where there's a farmers' market on Saturdays offering yet more organic bounty. Daylesford has other London outlets in Notting Hill (208-212 Westbourne Grove, W11), Marylebone (6-8 Blandford Street, W1) and Selfridges (see page 81).

Daylesford Organic, 44B Pimlico Rd, SW1W 8LP (020-7881 8060; http://daylesford.com/locations; Sloane Sq tube; Mon-Sat 8am-8pm, Sun 10am-4pm).

E5 Bakehouse

An organic bakery – best sourdough in London – and coffee shop in East London (E8, confusingly), the E5 Bakehouse is built into an archway with tables outside for warmer days. The staff have a passion for hand-crafted sourdough bread and the 'lost' traditions of baking, using traditional techniques and natural ingredients: locally-sourced organic flour, water and sea salt. Apart from their baguettes, ciabatta and foccacia, all loaves are made from 100 per cent sourdough starters, which means they are leavened entirely from wild yeast and bacteria starter dough refreshed daily.

The E5's bakers share their knowledge and expertise in bread-making classes suitable for all skill levels.

E5 Bakehouse, Arch 395, Mentmore Ter, E8 3PH (020-8525 2890; http://e5bakehouse.com; London Fields rail; Mon-Wed 9am-5pm, Thu-Sun 9am-6pm).

FarmW5

The folks behind FarmW5 have a passion for organic food, working in partnership with over 50 small UK growers and producers. All produce on sale at the Ealing shop is certified organic or slow food (see www.slowfood.com).

FarmW5 claim that everything they sell is 'simply the best' (no false modesty here!), including meat and poultry from organic farms in Somerset and Cornwall; fish from sustainable stocks landed in Looe and Brixham; mushrooms from Winchester; and honey from just round the corner in Ealing. There's a coffee and juice bar too.

FarmW5, 19 The Green, W5 5DA (020-8566 1965; www.farmw5.co.uk; Ealing Broadway rail; Mon-Fri 8am-7.30pm, Sat 9am-7pm, Sun 11am-5pm).

Food Halls

The food halls of London's top department stores deserve a special mention, offering the best of British alongside produce from all corners of the globe. Designed to tempt you at every turn, their counters groan with luxury foods: artisan cheeses, caviar, exotic charcuterie, luxury chocolates, truffles, foie gras…

Fortnum & Mason: This world-famous emporium in Piccadilly is a compelling combination of delicatessen, department store (see page 73), restaurant and living museum. Founded as a grocery store, Fortnum's reputation was built on supplying top-quality food, and its fame grew rapidly throughout the Victorian era. Over the centuries it has developed into a department store, although its fame rests mostly on its food hall situated on the lower ground and ground floors.

Harrods: London's most famous store (see page 74) boasts an Art Nouveau food hall that's a tourist attraction in its own right. The opulent rooms are more salon than supermarket, from the mosaic frieze and lovely tile-work depicting farming and hunting scenes, to the chandeliers sparkling off the stained glass ceilings. The glorious décor makes a wonderful backdrop for the artful displays of mouth-watering gourmet food, noted for its variety, quality and luxury – and eye-watering prices!

Harvey Nichols: Although it's best known for its fashionable clothes and accessories, Harvey Nichols (see page 75) has a stellar reputation for its on-trend food. The fifth-floor Foodmarket at the Knightsbridge store vividly illustrates Harvey Nicks' commitment to high-quality, carefully-sourced, great-

London's grand food halls cater to shoppers with very deep pockets. For most of us they're places to buy a special treat, rather than do the weekly shop.

tasting food. It boasts an impressive range of national and international produce from many of the world's very best suppliers. There are regular tasting evenings and product launches too.

demonstrations and tastings. Every possible cuisine is represented (raw ingredients, artisan and prepared foods) from all corners of the globe,

including Persian caviar, succulent jamón ibérico, fresh lobster, Wagyu beef, biltong, exotic spices and much more.

John Lewis: The food hall at John Lewis' Oxford Street store (see page 77) is operated by Waitrose – 'quality food, honestly priced' – a division of the John Lewis Partnership and the foodies' favourite supermarket chain. It occupies most of the vast basement and is a paradise for food lovers, bursting with fresh seasonal produce and inviting artisan foods. It also provides a home delivery and party service and online shopping.

Selfridges: Selfridges (see page 81) sells all manner of edible treats and is noted for its vast range and superb quality. It's a honey pot for serious cooks and a great place to keep abreast of the latest food trends, which are promoted through

La Fromagerie

Widely recognised as one of London's (and the UK's) best cheese shops, La Fromagerie is a firm favourite with chefs, gourmets and foodies. Patricia and Danny Michelson opened their first shop in Highbury in 1992, and the Moxon Street outlet followed ten years later; both feature special cellars with on-site *affinage* (for ageing and maturing cheese) and signature walk-in cheese rooms.

They specialise in farmhouse cheeses, both regional British and European, sourced directly from artisan producers and carefully matured to peak condition. There's also a floor dedicated to other well-sourced produce, including seasonal fruit and vegetables, freshly-baked bread, extra virgin olive oils and vinegars, and other essential dry store ingredients and condiments. The on-site kitchen produces preserves and chutneys, biscuits and cakes, along with a daily changing menu of food to take away or enjoy in the café, a welcome respite from London's busy streets. Usefully, the shop is next door to the acclaimed Ginger Pig butcher (see page 134).

La Fromagerie has an excellent website with advice on creating the perfect cheese plate – and even choosing wines to go with it!

La Fromagerie, 2-6 Moxon St, W1U 4EW (020-7935 0341; www.lafromagerie.co.uk; Baker St tube; Mon-Fri 8am-7.30pm, Sat 9am-7pm, Sun 10am-6pm).

R Garcia & Sons

Established in 1958 amid the bustle of Portobello Road, Garcia's is London's largest and best Spanish grocer and delicatessen. It's worth visiting just for its excellent charcuterie counter, offering a mouth-watering selection of top-quality Spanish cured hams and sausages, including jamón ibérico and serrano ham, *morcilla* (a type of Spanish black pudding), spicy chorizo sausage, salted pork ribs and tasty salamis.

There's a comprehensive selection of Spanish cheeses, including Minorcan mahón, tetilla from Galicia and the ever-popular manchego, plus an abundance of olives, olive oil, sherry vinegar, preserves, paella rice, almonds, pistachios, dried beans, tins of snails and jars of *boquerones* (anchovies), herbs and spices, sweets (try the turrón) and much more. Not forgetting a splendid selection of Spanish wine, sherry, cava and brandy. Garcia's has all the ingredients you need to produce authentic tapas or a full-blown Spanish banquet, plus free advice on tap from the friendly staff.

You can whet your appetite at Café Garcia or at one of the local Spanish eateries. Try an authentic cortado coffee, hot chocolate and churros, or a few tapas with a glass of fino. *¡Buen provecho!*

R Garcia & Sons, 248-250 Portobello Rd, W11 1LL (020-7221 6119; http://rgarciaandsons.com; Ladbroke Grove tube; Sun-Mon 10am-6pm, Tue-Sat 9am-6pm).

Ginger Pig

The Ginger Pig began over 20 years ago with a near-derelict farmhouse and three Tamworth pigs, and now farms over 3,000 acres of its own pasture and moorland in North Yorkshire, as well as working with a network of like-minded farmers. At the heart of the business is good animal husbandry and welfare: happy pigs taste better!

There are seven London outlets (Barnes, Borough Market, Clapham, Hackney, Marylebone, Shepherds Bush and Waterloo) – we have chosen to feature the Hackney branch. GP is the city's most celebrated butcher and where many of its top chefs and restaurants buy their meat, choosing from a mind-boggling range of products, including beef, lamb, chicken and duck, as well as pork.

The Hackney outlet is small but perfectly formed, situated in Victoria Park village, home to cafés, restaurants, pubs and a fishmonger. In addition to the usual butchery

counter there's a selection of cured meats, cold cuts, chutneys and dry goods, plus Ginger Pig's celebrated sausage rolls and pies – including their famous tiered pork pie cake, perfect for a carnivore's celebration. And if you want to improve your knife skills, you can sign up for a range of butchery classes.

The Ginger Pig, 99 Lauriston Rd, E9 7HJ (020-8986 6911; www.thegingerpig.co.uk; Homerton rail/Bethnal Grn tube; Mon-Wed 9am-5.30pm, Thu-Fri 9am-6.30pm, Sat 9am-6pm, Sun 10am-3pm).

A. Gold

and toffee from Cumbria, Campbell's tea and Camp coffee, sugar mice and hand-made fudge, Stinking Bishop cheese, English mead, Dorset knobs (a type of biscuit), Cornish gingerbread, London honey, Henderson's relish, lemon curd, cream soda, sloe gin, gooseberry wine, brandy snaps and much, much more. Or you can buy a hamper and indulge your every whim. Gold's takeaway food service includes excellent coffee, imaginative sandwiches, traditional pies and their famous scotch eggs.

A. Gold, 42 Brushfield St, E1 6AG (020-7247 2487; www.agoldshop.com; Liverpool St tube/rail; Mon-Fri 10am-4pm, Sat-Sun 11am-5pm).

Looking like an old-fashioned grocer and styling itself as 'a village shop in the City', A. Gold is somewhere you can buy a cup of slow-brewed Monmouth coffee, a bag of traditional sweets or a homemade scotch egg. Located in busy Spitalfields (next door to Verde & Co – see page 150), it's the only deli in London to offer entirely British produce, championing small independent producers from across the UK. Founded in 2000 by Ian and Safia Thomas – the name comes from milliner Amelia Gold, one of the building's former residents – it was taken over by Philip Cundall and Paulo Garcia in 2010 and has since gone from strength to strength.

This Aladdin's cave of a shop offers a wealth of nostalgic treats, such as bacon

Greensmiths

Greensmiths is an example of how good a local supermarket can be if it puts provenance over profit and works in partnership with artisan producers. Established in 2008 by Chris Smith who wanted to create something special, Waterloo-based Greensmiths has been winning plaudits ever since for its combination of superb food, excellent service and stylish interior.

It looks small from the outside but is something of a Tardis, opening up to reveal a number of levels. As well as the products you'd expect to find – groceries, general goods and dairy goods, there's a cheesemonger plus a number of concessions (both producers and merchants) which include a butcher (The Ginger Pig – see page 134), a baker (The Old Post Office Bakery), a greengrocer

(Solstice), a coffee/beverages specialist (Caffe Antica) and a wine merchant (Waterloo Wine Company). Thus your shopping experience is seamless, with the advantage of being able to buy from specialists and profit from their expert advice – so much more satisfying than simply pushing a trolley around the aisles.

A range of delicious dishes is prepared in Greensmiths' kitchen to eat in the lovely café or take away – great prices too!

Greensmiths, 27 Lower Marsh, SE1 7RG (020-7921 2970; www.greensmithsfood.co.uk; Lambeth N or Waterloo tube; Mon-Fri 8am-8pm, Sat 8am-6pm, closed Sun).

Hampstead Butcher & Providore

Established in 2010 by entrepreneur Philip Matthews, with a team led by renowned chef Guy Bossom, the Hampstead Butcher & Providore was an immediate success. This foodie gem is Hampstead's premier butcher, delicatessen, charcuterie, cheese and wine shop, offering an extensive range of meat and poultry, sausages and hams, pates, marinades and savoury snacks, many of which are made on the premises. There's a second shop in West Hampstead (244 West End Lane). HB&P also stocks an extensive range of larder essentials from artisan suppliers.

It's a sociable venue, with regular tastings, dinners, events and even butchery classes. A genuine local treasure.

The Hampstead Butcher & Providore, 56 Rosslyn Hill, NW3 1ND (020-7794 9210; www. hampsteadbutcher.com; Hampstead tube; Mon-Sat 9am-7pm, Sun 9am-6pm).

Leila's Shop

Leila's (owned by Leila McAlister) is a bijou gem in Shoreditch; a combination of old-fashioned grocer and modern café. Farm-fresh fruit and veg is displayed outside in woven baskets, wooden crates and glazed bowls, while the rustic interior is piled high with seasonal produce and store-cupboard goodies: bread, cheese, butter, eggs, olive oil, almonds, juices, chutneys, jams, gourmet coffee, leaf tea and much more.

After you've restocked your larder, you can pop into the café next door for coffee, lunch or a delicious breakfast/brunch – try Leila's signature dish of fried eggs with sage or crisp-fried serrano ham (served in a cast-iron frying pan) and sourdough toast.

Leila's Shop, 15-17 Calvert Ave, E2 7JN (020-7729 9789; Bethnal Grn tube; Wed-Sat 10am-6pm, Sun 10am-5pm, Mon-Tue closed).

Lina Stores

This family-run Italian deli with its classic '50s green ceramic frontage is a landmark in Soho, where it has been trading since 1944. Although spruced up in recent years, Lina Stores has lost none of its rustic charm. Its centrepiece is a huge marble and green-tiled deli counter, surrounded by mouth-watering hams hanging from the rafters and shelves overflowing with tempting produce.

This iconic treasure house stocks all the essentials for *la dolce vita*, such as sauces (heavenly pesto and passata), breads, marinated artichokes, truffles, oils and olives. There's a splendid selection of cheeses, including taleggio, fresh buffalo mozzarella and *pecorino brigante* (sheep's cheese), and those famous meats: Parma ham, homemade Italian sausage and salamis such as *lardo* (salami cured with rosemary) and *finocchiona* (salami with fennel). However, Lina's is perhaps best known for its fresh pasta, especially ravioli and tortelloni, which customers travel miles to buy (cookery writer Jane Grigson was a famous customer). Classic fillings of spinach and ricotta or pumpkin jostle with specials such as porcini, artichoke and truffle oil, or pea and mint.

Cakes and desserts are baked on site, including the Italian classic *torta caprese* (chocolate and almond cake), panettone and mascarpone muffins, plus a selection of regional Italian wines.

Lina Stores, 18 Brewer St, W1F 0SH (020-7437 6482; https://linastores.co.uk; Piccadilly Circus tube; Mon-Tue 8.30am-7.30pm, Wed-Fri 8.30am-8.30pm, Sat 10am-7.30pm, Sun 11am-5pm).

Melrose & Morgan

Melrose & Morgan in chic Primrose Hill calls itself a 'grocery shop', although it certainly isn't your average corner shop but rather an outstanding gourmet delicatessen and café. This grocer-cum-kitchen supplies artisan products and ingredients, as well as freshly-prepared meals, for those who care about the quality of their food and its preparation and can afford to pay for the very best. Some two-thirds of M&M's food is made in-house in small batches and what they don't make themselves is carefully sourced from local artisans and independent retailers.

The Primrose Hill shop (their first outlet – there's a second in Hampstead) opened in 2004 and has a café where you can enjoy breakfast, lunch or tea, or pick up something for supper. As well as its freshly-cooked range of pies, soups, pastries, cakes and tarts, M&M sells a wealth of first-class produce, including organic and free-range meat and poultry, cheese, and everyday supplies such as milk, bread and juices. There are also hand-made chocolates, wines and oils, plus fresh fruit and vegetables.

It's a lot more expensive than Tesco, but that would be like comparing chalk and cheese when it comes to flavour and quality. You can order online too.

Melrose & Morgan, 42 Gloucester Ave, NW1 8JD (020-7722 0011; www.melroseandmorgan.com; Chalk Farm tube; Mon-Fri 8am-7pm, Sat 8am-6pm, Sun 9am-5pm).

Mr Christian's

A foodie institution, Mr Christian's delicatessen in Notting Hill was founded in 1974 by Tim Dawson and Glynn Christian. Glynn was one of the original TV chefs – on BBC1's *Pebble Mill at One* and later *BBC Breakfast Time* – and the shop soon had a devoted customer base. Gregg Scott later took over the business and in 2003 it became part of Jeroboams wine merchants group (www.jeroboams.co.uk). However, it remains a thriving foodie business that remains true to its founder's vision.

There's a great choice of quality products on offer, including unique cheeses and charcuterie, smoked fish, organic ice cream and own-label jams, pickles and honey, as well as home-cooked lunch dishes – such as roast butternut squash and goats' cheese risotto cakes – salads and sandwiches. Mr Christian's is particularly famous for its breads (it sells over 50 types) and pastries, including homemade sausage rolls, savoury pastries, sweet treats and freshly-made patisserie.

The deli stocks a range of top-quality basics such as French butter, crème fraîche, sea salt, herbs and spices, organic milk and free-range eggs, mustards, chutneys, marinades, oils, vinegars, dips, organic teas, coffee, chocolates and much more.

Mr Christian's, 11 Elgin Cres, W11 2JA (020-7229 0501; www.mrchristians.co.uk; Ladbroke Grove tube; Mon-Sat 7.30am-6pm, Sun 8am-3pm).

Moxon's

Fishmonger Robin Moxon is regarded as one of the best in London, with four outlets: Clapham, East Dulwich, Islington and South Kensington – the one featured here. They sell ethically-caught fish sourced daily from London's Billingsgate Market (see page 200) and suppliers around the UK, including some in Newlyn and Plymouth in Cornwall, Brixham in Devon, Peterhead and Loch Duart in Scotland, Scalloway in the Shetland Islands and Newhaven in Sussex.

monkfish, mullet, plaice, rock salmon, smoked mackerel, tuna, turbot, plus wild smoked salmon and sea bass, while the choice of shellfish encompasses clams, crab, lobster, mussels, oysters, scallops and more. The friendly staff are happy to offer advice and prepare fish to suit your needs, and you can also browse a library of cookbooks for inspiration. The shop stocks a range of fish-friendly accompaniments such as samphire and store-cupboard goods.

Moxon's, 17 Bute St, SW7 3EY (020-7591 0050; www.moxonsfreshfish.com; S Kensington tube; Tue-Fri 8.30am-7.30pm, Sat 8.30am-5.30pm, closed Sun-Mon).

Moxon's sells a comprehensive range of fish and shellfish, with the emphasis on freshness and seasonality. Depending on the time of year, you can buy Cornish bream, Dover sole, halibut, herring,

The Natural Kitchen

The Natural Kitchen in Marylebone (with six other outlets including Baker Street, Fetter Lane and Trinity Square) is a high-class food emporium founded in 2007 and now operating as a deli with a café/juice bar upstairs. It sells artisan, organic and wild food – ethical foods, sustainably sourced – supplied by the likes of River Cottage, Paxton & Whitfield (cheese) and Vintage Roots (alcoholic and non-alcoholic organic tipples).

The Natural Kitchen's speciality is high quality free-range meat and poultry, sourced (where possible) directly from small traditional farms, such as Monkshill Farm in Kent which supplies salt marsh lamb, 'Kentish Ranger' free-range chickens, and pork from Oxford sandy and black pigs. Butchers Andy and John (www.chefandbutcher.co.uk) are happy to proffer

expert advice on choosing and cooking their quality meats.

If you're short on time or cooking skills, a tasty range of ready-to-cook dishes is available such as chicken Kiev, veal and basil meatballs and salt marsh lamb koftas, while the 'Food to Go' counters offer a large choice of seasonal salads, quiches, soups, pies and sandwiches, plus a range of drinks.

The Natural Kitchen, 77-78 Marylebone High St, W1U 5JX (020-7486 8065 deli or 020-7935 9822 butcher; www.thenaturalkitchen.com; Baker St tube; Mon-Fri 7am-8pm, Sat 8am-7pm, Sun 9am-7pm).

Neal's Yard Dairy

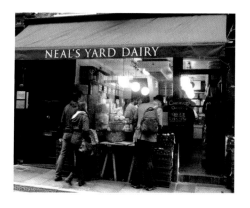

Neal's Yard Dairy has been providing Londoners with fresh cheese and other dairy produce since 1979, and now supplies shops and restaurants around the world. It buys from some 70 British and Irish cheesemakers and sells the produce in its stores in Borough Market, Bermondsey and Neal's Yard (Covent Garden). The business maintains close contact with its cheesemakers, visiting them regularly, and it's this attention to detail that has made Neal's Yard a byword for top-quality cheese.

Many of the cheeses are either matured on the farm or in the dairy's maturing rooms in Bermondsey, located in brick railway arches under the main line from London Bridge to Dover. The insulation provided by the venerable Victorian brickwork helps maintain excellent conditions for the cheeses – humid and cool – which are meticulously nurtured until they reach peak condition. Neal's Yard also has its own creamery at Dorstone Hill (overlooking the Wye Valley in Herefordshire), where it makes Greek-style and strained Greek yoghurt, goat's curd and some splendid goat's milk cheeses.

Neal's Yard runs various cheese classes at its Bermondsey warehouse, where the experienced team guide you through a tasting of traditional and modern artisan cheeses with liquid accompaniments.

Neal's Yard Dairy, 17 Shorts Gdns, WC2H 9AT (020-7240 5700; www.nealsyarddairy.co.uk; Covent Gdn tube; Mon-Sat 10am-7pm, closed Sun).

Oliver's Wholefoods Store

Oliver's is an award-winning neighbourhood store sourcing the best organic foods from small local producers. It was established in 1989 by ex-chef Sara Novakovic, previously employed at the Institute for Advanced Nutrition. Sara believes strongly in the close link between good health and natural foods, and much of the produce sold at Oliver's is organic, including fresh fruit and veg, fish, meat, cheese, juices, local honey, bread, dried goods and wine.

The store also caters for special diets, selling wheat- and gluten-free foods, along with natural and homeopathic remedies, nutritional supplements and bodycare products. There's even an in-store nutritionist.

Oliver's Wholefoods Store, 5 Station Approach, TW9 3QB (020-8948 3990; www. oliverswholefoods.co.uk; Kew Gdns tube; Mon-Sat 9am-8.30pm, Sun 10am-8.30pm).

Partridges

Established in 1972, Partridges is one of only a handful of family-run food emporiums remaining in central London. One of London's poshest food stores (with a royal warrant), it's up there with Fortnum & Mason and Harrods' Food Hall (only smaller) – as are the prices! You'll find everything you need to entertain royally (or royalty!), from duck liver paté to truffles, beluga caviar to oysters, Belgian hand-made chocolates to exotic teas and coffee. There's also a superb selection of vintage champagnes and fine wines, plus a wine bar and café. There's also a rather posh food market (see page 215) held every Saturday in Duke of York Square.

Partridges, 2-5 Duke of York Sq, SW3 4LY (020-7730 0651; www.partridges.co.uk; Sloane Sq; daily 8am-10pm).

The People's Supermarket

The People's Supermarket is a sustainable, environmentally-friendly, non-profit co-operative established in 2010 to provide the people of WC1 with good food at fair prices. Although anyone can shop at the store, you can become a member for an annual fee of £25, although you must commit to working in the shop for four hours each month (no experience required). In return you receive a 20 per cent discount off food purchases and a say in how the shop is run. A spin-off, the People's Kitchen, offers food to take away.

The People's Supermarket, 72-76 Lamb's Conduit St, WC1N 3LP (020-7430 1827; http:// thepeoplessupermarket.org; Russell Sq tube; Mon-Sat 8am-9pm, Sun 10am-6pm).

The People's Supermarket

Persepolis

Co-owned by the indomitable Sally Butcher, Persepolis in Peckham is much more than a food shop – it's an cornucopia of all things Persian, from samovars to shisha pipes. But don't let the handicrafts distract you; this charming shop is a serious foodie haven. It's packed to the rafters with exotic foods, including fresh dates, preserved limes, dried lemons, exotic herbs and spices (such as *sumak* and *za'atar*), pomegranate molasses, rosewater, stuffed vine leaves, sour cherries, baklava and much more.

There's also a café serving excellent mezze dishes and much more. Sally is the author of half a dozen celebrated cookbooks (see the excellent website for information).

Persepolis, 28-30 Peckham High St, SE15 5DT (020-7639 8007; www.foratasteofpersia.co.uk; Peckham Rye rail; daily 10.35am-9pm).

Philglas & Swiggot

Founded in 1991 in Clapham, Philglas & Swiggot (geddit?) is one of London's most exciting wine merchants (London Wine Merchant of the Year 2002-06). The owner is an Aussie, therefore it's no surprise that it majors in Antipodean wines, but it also stocks one of the city's best selections of Italian, regional French, Californian and Spanish wines.

And it's a great place to seek out less well-known wines from Austria, Hungary, Portugal and further afield. Now with three outlets (Clapham, Marylebone and Richmond), its mission is to bring the world's more interesting and innovative wines to its customers – which it does in spades.

Philglas & Swiggot, 21 Northcote Rd, SW11 1NG (020-7924 4494; www.philglas-swiggot.com; Clapham Jct tube/rail; Mon-Fri 11am-8pm, Sat 10am-7pm, Sun noon-5pm).

Phoenicia Mediterranean Food Hall

Founded in 2003, the Phoenicia Mediterranean Food Hall in north London is a family-run business and a labour of love. It specialises in high-quality food from the Eastern Med – Greece, Italy, Lebanon, Morocco and Turkey – especially products that are difficult to find elsewhere at reasonable prices, such as *freekah* (green wheat, made popular by Ottolenghi). There's a delicatessen stocked with marvellous mezze dishes like *tabbouleh* and *baba ganoush*; mouth-watering handmade bread, cakes and pastries (including Turkish pita and fresh baklava); a superb halal butcher; fantastic olives and olive oil; and much more. There's also a café that sells great wraps.

Phoenicia Mediterranean Food Hall, 186-192 Kentish Town Rd, NW5 2AE (020-7267 1267; www.phoeniciafoodhall.co.uk; Kentish Town tube; Mon-Sat 9am-8pm, Sun 10am-6pm).

Postcard Teas

Postcard Teas in Dering Street (just off Oxford Street) is at the forefront of the capital's renewed fascination with tea, from sampling unusual and exotic leaves to taking afternoon tea. It's the brainchild of Timothy d'Offay whose fascination for tea and tea culture was nurtured when he lived in Kyoto (Japan) over 20 years ago. Since then his passion has taken him throughout Asia and his knowledge of tea is immense.

This postcard-sized shop stocks rare teas from across the globe and specialises in 'small tea', i.e. sustainably produced leaves from small, family-owned farms that produce tea (among other crops), ideally without hired help. Surprisingly, these small producers are responsible for over half the tea in Asia, and all authentic examples of the most famous teas of China, Japan, Korea, Taiwan and Vietnam are grown by 'small tea' specialists. Every packet of tea sold by Postcard Teas contains its provenance, so you'll know exactly where it was grown.

On Saturdays at 10am (before the shop officially opens) Tim hosts a relaxed one-hour tea tasting (booking essential) complete with illustrated tasting notes. Whether your taste is for black, white, green or blue (e.g. aromatic Oolong) tea, you'll be spoilt for choice at Postcard Teas. There's also an excellent website for tea aficionados.

Postcard Teas, 9 Dering St, W1S 1AG (020-7629 3654; www.postcardteas.com; Bond St tube; Mon-Fri 10.30am-6.30pm, Sat 11am-6.30pm, closed Sun).

The Spice Shop

The Spice Shop has been a fixture on the Notting Hill shopping scene since the '90s. It began life as a market stall on Portobello Road to supplement owner Birgit Erath's income while she was studying at university, and moved into the shop in 1995, since when Birgit's fame as a spice trader has spread far and wide. Today it offers a range of more than 2,500 products and is the only one of its kind in the UK, frequented by famous chefs and TV cooks who draw upon Birgit's knowledge as a source of inspiration and recipe ideas.

As well as all the staples, the Spice Shop stocks an astounding variety of the more exotic and esoteric spices from lemon myrtle to medieval ginger. There are sections devoted to fresh herbs, chillies, paprika, flavoured salts and peppercorns, plus Birgit's own herb and spice mixes. You can also order online and have spices delivered anywhere in the world.

As well as running the shop, Birgit teaches at local bookshop Books for Cooks (see page 34), advises major food corporations, and has even found time to co-author a book (*Barbecue*) about 'fire-powered' barbecue food.

The Spice Shop, 1 Blenheim Cres, W11 2EE (020-7221 4448; www.thespiceshop.co.uk; Ladbroke Grove tube; Mon-Sat 9.30am-6pm, Sun 11am-4pm).

Tavola

Tavola is an outstanding Italian deli in west London – run by former top chef and television celebrity Alastair Little and his wife Sharon – which defines London food culture. Out front there's a colourful display of fruit and veg such as artichokes, aubergines, fennel, lemons, peppers and plum tomatoes, while inside the shelves overflow with balsamic vinegar and virgin olive oil, jars of French fish soup, haricot beans, olives, risotto rice and Italian pearled spelt (*farro*), truffle paste, pasta in every shape and size, Valrhona chocolate and wonderful Italian breads.

The centre of the shop is given over to cooked foods: scarlet peppers stuffed with white mozzarella, squelchy braised fennel, chicken liver pâté and braised rabbit. Little also produces some of the best pasta sauces in London, such as pesto alla Genovese, a rabbit sauce for pappardelle and a rich beef ragu. And to complete the

authentic Italian table, there's a display of exquisitely painted Italian pottery, superior cookware and crisp linen napkins. Tavola has no coffee or sandwich service, nowhere to sit and no mail order service – it's simply an old-fashioned deli offering fantastic food.

Tavola, 155 Westbourne Grove, W11 2RS (020-7229 0571; www.tavolalondon.co.uk; Notting Hill Gate tube; Mon-Fri 10am-7.30pm, Sat 10am-6pm, closed Sun).

Verde & Company

This traditional grocery shop in Spitalfields is a 19th-century treasure trove stocked with 21st-century edible luxuries. The building is owned by writer Jeanette Winterson – who's keen to maintain the area's traditional Georgian atmosphere – while the old-fashioned grocery is the inspiration of chef-proprietor Harvey Cabaniss. The shop retains all the charm of yesteryear, enhanced with a lovely display of antique china, Staffordshire figures, toy theatres and 19th-century clocks, but sells food that's bang up to date with the latest foodie culture: fresh, natural and artisan. It's an up-market foodie mecca with an emphasis on Italian food.

V&C is packed to the rafters with Harvey's favourite deli treats such as Belgian Pierre Marcolini chocolates, fresh pasta, homemade preserves, fine olive oils and

balsamic vinegars. It also offers a selection of homemade cakes and pastries and a range of delicious salads and sandwiches, such as bresaola with sun-blush tomatoes; chorizo with Gorgonzola and sweet chilli; goat's cheese with grilled aubergine; and suckling pig with piquillo peppers. Food is available to take away (delivery available) and there are even some seats for the lucky few.

Verde & Company, 40 Brushfield St, E1 6AG (020-7247 1924; www.verdeandco.co.uk; Shoreditch High St tube; Mon-Thu 9am-9pm, Fri 9am-6pm, Sat-Sun 10am-6pm).

Whole Foods Market

Part of the largest organic food chain in the US, the Whole Foods Market has five UK food emporiums (four in London), of which the Kensington outlet (housed in the former Barkers department store) is the largest, extending to some 80,000ft^2. Everything here is organic and/or locally sourced, free from artificial preservatives, colourings, flavourings, sweeteners and hydrogenated fats. The store offers a vast choice of products – including 100 different olive oils, 40 types of sausage and 50 fresh juices – from fruit and vegetables to meat and dairy products, and is one of the finest organic retailers in London.

The market also offers a wide range of eating options from a number of different food venues, including oven-baked pizza, dim sum, sushi, a trattoria and wok station, Texas BBQ, soup, salads, burritos and tacos, along with vegetarian and vegan options and a juice bar. There's also a wine hub and bar with wines available by the glass.

Much more than just a food retailer, there's a health and beauty department on the lower ground floor devoted to natural skincare and supplements, plus treatment rooms offering facials, skin care analysis, manicures, massages, nutritional advice, holistic treatments, homeopathic remedies and even yoga.

Whole Foods Market, The Barkers Building, 63-97 Kensington High St, W8 5SE (020-7368 4500; www.wholefoodsmarket.com/stores/kensington; High St Kensington tube; Mon-Sat 8am-10pm, Sun noon-6pm).

Pitfield London

7.

Furniture & Homeware

Y ou can buy good furniture throughout the UK, but for sheer choice London is hard to beat. The vast city hosts a multitude of places offering things for your home, from beautiful bespoke designs and rare antiques to cheap and cheerful contemporary furniture and functional vintage pieces. Naturally your choice will depend on your budget (and taste), but good design needn't cost the earth.

This chapter features over 30 of London's best independent furniture, homeware and design outlets, scattered liberally around the city from Brompton Road to Tottenham Court Road, Islington to Shoreditch, where you can buy everything from state-of-the-art cookware to snazzy sofas. Many pieces are cutting-edge designs that are set to be the antiques of tomorrow, while others are simply just fun.

We've also included some household names, such as Habitat and Heal's, as well as the major department stores which offer a wealth of styles and prices under one roof. And for those on a shoestring budget there are always London's markets (see **Chapter 9**) and car-boot sales, where you can pick up unloved treasures for a song and find nondescript furniture just waiting to be upcycled into something of beauty. (See also **Chapter 1** for antique, vintage and retro home ideas.)

Aram

Zeev Aram opened his first furniture showroom – a small white space on London's King's Road – in 1964. This was long before the British began to embrace modern design, and Aram was out on a retail limb, stocking pieces by Breuer, Castiglioni and Le Corbusier. Today his business occupies a vast five-storey warehouse in Covent Garden and is one of the capital's top destinations for modern furniture, lighting and homeware. The store is a treasure house of contemporary design where you can invest in everything from Zeev's beloved Castiglioni Toio lamp to a prototype by an unknown designer fresh out of college.

Aram, 110 Drury Ln, WC2B 5SG (020-7557 7557; www.aram.co.uk; Covent Gdn tube; Mon-Wed, Fri-Sat 10am-6pm, Thu 10am-7pm, closed Sun).

Aria

At the cutting edge of home and fashion for over two decades, Aria is located in Islington's atmospheric Barnsbury Hall, where the building's original 1850s features contrast beautifully with the über-modern lines of Aria's wares. On sale is an eclectic range of contemporary home furnishings and lifestyle accessories, alongside selected vintage pieces and collaborations with local designers. Here you can pick up a pastel-coloured pebble stool, a funky tongue chair or, if the budget doesn't stretch quite that far, a simple table lamp, retro radio or chic candle set.

The design-orientated lifestyle store offers everything from fashion to jewellery, cosmetics and toiletries. There's a café, too.

Aria, Barnsbury Hall, Barnsbury St, N1 1PN (020-7704 6222; www.ariashop.co.uk; Essex Rd rail/ Angel tube; Mon-Sat 10am-6.30pm, Sun noon-5pm).

Atelier Abigail Ahern

This little jewel box of a store was founded in 2003 by Abigail Ahern, an internationally renowned designer, style icon and author of a number of books, including *Decorating with Style* (2013). The store's eclectic wares include gargoyles made from granite and sandstone, beautiful artificial flowers, marble flower vases in the form of clenched fists, a large zebra head fashioned from beads and faux zebra rugs.

Abigail is internationally renowned for her uncompromising taste and trendsetting designs which are synonymous with glamour and humour, and has a global following through her influential blog, product designs and store, voted one of the coolest places to shop by *Elle Decoration*.

Atelier Abigail Ahern, 137 Upper St, N1 1QP (020-7354 8181; http://abigailahern.com; Essex Rd Rail/Angel tube; Mon-Sat 10.30am-6pm, Sun noon-5pm).

Chaplins

Since opening its doors over 20 years ago, family-run Chaplins has been showcasing the very best in contemporary design and style at its vast 25,000ft^2 showroom in Hatch End. The store features a huge range of glamorous room sets and individual products highlighting cutting-edge interior design and modern living from major contemporary furniture manufacturers, plus lighting, art and a wide range of homeware accessories. There's everything from couches to clocks to chandeliers. Chaplins has forged partnerships and close relationships with many top designers and contemporary brands, and also offers a comprehensive interior design service.

Chaplins, 477-507 Uxbridge Rd, HA5 4JS (020-8421 1779; http://chaplins.co.uk; Hatch End rail; Mon-Sat 10am-6pm, closed Sun).

The Conran Shop

F ounded in 1974 by Terence Conran –
who pioneered British modernism in
the '60s (see **Habitat** on page 162) – the
Conran Shop's flagship store (opened in
1987) occupies part of the iconic Michelin
House building on Fulham Road in Chelsea.
Commissioned by the Michelin Tyre
Company and opened in 1911, the building
was designed at the end of the Art Nouveau
period, but with its strong advertising images
it's more like an Art Deco building, albeit one
20 years ahead of its time.

The Conran Shop offers a collection
of furniture, lighting, kitchen and dining
products, home accessories and gifts from
some of the most iconic designers and up-
and-coming talent from around the globe.
Simple functionality, considered design and
the latest innovation are the foundation

of Conran's philosophy. Store highlights
include the enchanting child shop (complete
with playroom and party essentials), a
covetable range of bags and accessories,
and a zen-like spa room offering exclusive
beauty and grooming products. *Homes &
Gardens* magazine's Retailer of the Year in
2013, the Conran Shop continues to play a
central role in the flourishing London design
scene.

The building also houses the critically-
acclaimed Bibendum Restaurant, named
after Michelin's iconic figure, Monsieur
Bibendum, aka the 'Michelin Man'.

**Conran Shop, Michelin House, 81 Fulham Rd,
SW3 6RD (020-7589 7401; www.conranshop.
co.uk; S Kensington tube; Mon-Tue, Fri 10am-
6pm, Wed-Thu 10am-7pm, Sat 10am-6.30pm, Sun
noon-6pm).**

Darlings of Chelsea

A small chain of six UK stores (plus one in Verbier, Switzerland), Darlings of Chelsea's flagship (and original) showroom is located on Fulham High Street. They are famous for their bespoke handcrafted sofas and chairs – mostly British-made – including corner sofas, sofa beds and armchairs, although their product range also extends to beds, rugs and cushions, lighting, homeware

and more. One of the most respected names in the sofa business, Darlings offer a comprehensive range of fabric and heritage English leather sofas, classic Chesterfields, a chic Italian range, and a designer collection including Duresta and Content by Conran.

From the classic wing back to the contemporary recliner, Darlings offers an exceptional range of chairs, including deep-seated tubs, leather study chairs and exclusive designer pieces. They're also noted for their wide choice of beds, particularly sofa beds in which they are market leaders. There's also an outstanding collection of lampshades, table lamps and light fittings, including an imaginative

selection from top lighting brand Ebb & Flow, plus a wide range of Clarke & Clarke cushions, which come in a variety of stylish colours, designs and shapes, and a selection of gorgeous rugs and carpets.

Darlings of Chelsea, 9-13 Fulham High St, SW6 3JH (020-7371 5745; www.darlingsofchelsea. co.uk; Putney Br tube; Mon-Thu 9am-6pm, Fri 9am-5pm, Sat 10am-5pm, Sun 11am-5pm).

Department Stores

London's department stores (see Chapter 4) are noted for their excellent furniture and homeware departments, which run the whole gamut of price, quality and design, from affordable mass-produced collections to eye-wateringly expensive bespoke contemporary and classic reproduction

designs. Whatever you're after, it will pay you handsomely to shop during the sales – which you can do online – when many items are reduced by up to 50 per cent.

Debenhams, House of Fraser and Marks & Spencer offer a wide range of good value contemporary and traditional furniture and furnishings, including own-brand designs, while John Lewis, Peter Jones and Selfridges also stock affordable ranges, along with more upmarket and exclusive pieces – John Lewis has the UK's largest home department at 94,000ft². Liberty is famous for its exclusive homeware collections, including beautiful fabrics, bed linen, wallpaper, curtains, cushions and throws, Eastern objets, kitchen- and tableware, lighting, rugs and carpets.

If money is no object, head for Harrods' massive furniture department, which boasts an unrivalled range of the world's most luxurious brands and most coveted designers. It showcases over 70 brands to suit every style and design taste, ranging from the ornately traditional to the ultra-modern and contemporary, including many exclusive limited-edition pieces.

Many department stores also offer a comprehensive interior design service.

See Chapter 4 for addresses and contact details.

The Design Centre

The Design Centre at Chelsea Harbour is a powerhouse of interior design, fully committed to inspiring, informing and delivering the best in design, both for professionals (such as interior designers and architects) and the general public. The Centre offers a unique shopping experience, with over 100 showrooms spread across some 145,000ft² of space, showcasing more than 500 of the world's most prestigious international interior design brands – it's the largest store of its kind in Europe and a leading design destination.

Synonymous with great design, it isn't surprising that every aspect of the Design Centre has been conceived to create the ultimate environment, with spectacular glass domes flooded with natural light and sleek curved glass balustrades.

From classic contemporary to cutting-edge cool under one roof, the Centre brings together fabrics, wall coverings, furniture, lighting, accessories, kitchen, bathroom, paint, outdoor living, curtain poles, hardware, tiles, carpets and more, with many showrooms offering a bespoke service for those seeking something unique. It's the perfect place to discover world-class talent, connect with influential designers and get the inside track on high profile events and design lectures (see website for details). There's also a design bookshop and a cool café.

Design Centre, Chelsea Harbour, Lots Rd, SW10 0XE (020-7225 9166; www.dcch.co.uk; Imperial Wharf rail; Mon-Fri 9.30am-5.30pm, closed Sat-Sun).

Design Museum Shop

As a city that's famous for its wealth of creative industries, it's only fitting that London should have a dedicated Design Museum. Originally housed in a former banana warehouse overlooking the Thames, the museum is due to move to the Commonwealth Institute Building in Kensington in late 2016 (see website for information).

The museum shop sells a unique selection of classic, beautiful, new and cutting-edge furniture, and objects focusing on architecture and all aspects of design from graphic design to fashion. Most merchandise is relevant to the museum's collections, exhibitions and installations, such as Cycle Revolution (some fab ideas for bike buffs) and the London Collection (secure your gift with London Skyline sticky tape!).

Design Museum, The Parabola, 224-238 Kensington High St, W8 6NQ (http://designmuseumshop.com; Kensington High St tube; see website for opening times).

Designers Guild

Founded in 1970 by Tricia Guild, the Designers Guild designs and sells its furnishing fabrics, wall coverings, upholstery, and bed and bath collections worldwide. At the King's Road Homestore and Showroom in Chelsea it offers exclusive products designed in its own studios alongside a huge range of contemporary and vintage accessories and gifts sourced from around

the world: tableware, linens, glassware, one-off studio ceramics, glass, fashion accessories, jewellery, rugs, garden products and toiletries. The collection comprises the best of contemporary and modern furniture and accessories from France, Italy and Scandinavia, including an extensive range from leading brands such as B&B Italia, Cappellini, Fritz Hansen, Knoll, Moroso and Vitra.

Designers Guild, 267-277 King's Rd, SW3 5EN (020-7351 5775; www.designersguild.com; Sloane Sq tube; Mon-Sat 10am-6pm, Sun noon-5pm, showroom closed Sundays).

Divertimenti

One of London's best (if not *the* best) cookshops, Divertimenti takes its name from the Italian *divertire* 'to entertain'. Its flagship store in Knightsbridge – there's another in Marylebone High Street – sells just about everything a keen cook could possibly need. The foodies' favourite since the '60s, it stocks over 6,500 items of professional quality cookware and tableware – including unique hand decorated pieces – cooking utensils, pots and pans, copper, earthenware, oriental utensils, cutlery, glassware, electrical appliances, cookers and cookbooks.

Divertimenti is also home to one of London's best cookery schools, with a range of classes for novice and experienced cooks alike. The school (located at the Brompton Road store) boasts a beautifully designed 'theatre' as well as a cookery 'island', where participants can learn from some of today's top chefs. Classes include demonstrations, hands-on masterclasses and even guided gastro tours including walks around Borough Market. The demos take in such diverse subjects as kosher food, celebration cakes, knife skills and even how to get the best out of your Aga, while hands-on classes include everything from sushi to sauces, pizza to dim sum.

Divertimenti also offers a range of services including wedding lists, copper pan re-tinning and professional knife sharpening.

Divertimenti, 227-229 Brompton Rd, SW3 2EP (020-7581 8065; www.divertimenti.co.uk; S Kensington tube; Mon-Tue, Thu-Fri 9.30am-6pm, Wed 9.30am-7pm, Sat 10am-6pm, Sun noon-5.30pm).

Feather & Black

Founded in 2004, Feather & Black have built an excellent reputation for their quality British-designed beds, bedroom furniture, storage solutions, mattresses, bed linen, towels, and bedroom accessories such as lamps, cushions, rugs, throws and clocks. The emphasis is on affordability, with a range of collections to suit all budgets and tastes, while designs range from earthy natural themes to chic loft living. With over 30 stores nationwide, frequent sales and a number of clearance stores (including branches in Chingford and Watford), Feather & Black offer a one-stop shop for all your bedroom needs.

Feather & Black, 83 Tottenham Court Rd, W1T 4SZ (020-7436 7707; www.featherandblack.com; Goodge St tube; Mon-Wed 10am-6pm, Thu 10am-8pm, Fri 10am-6.30pm, Sat 9.30am-6.30pm, Sun noon-6pm)

Habitat

Founded in 1964 by Terence Conran, Habitat has provided beautiful design at affordable prices for over 50 years; the name is synonymous with innovation, style and modern living. In its heyday it had more than 70 stores in the UK and abroad, but was a victim of recession, changing tastes and the rise of competitors such as IKEA.

In May 2016, the Sainsbury's supermarket chain was on course to take over Habitat's parent company Home Retail Group (who also owns Argos). Today, it has just three London stores, although there are mini Habitat stores in some branches of Homebase. Although diminished, the company continues to offer a unique collection of inexpensive but stylish furniture and home accessories, most of which are designed in-house.

Habitat, 196-199 Tottenham Court Rd, W1T 7PJ (0344-499 1122; www.habitat.co.uk; Goodge St tube; Mon-Wed, Fri-Sat 10am-7pm, Thu 10am-8pm, Sun noon-6pm).

Heal's

Founded in 1810 by John Harris Heal, Heal's has been a fixture on Tottenham Court Road since 1818. Its flagship store has occupied the iconic Heal's Building since it was completed in 1854. One of

the West End's most architecturally important buildings, it was designed in Venetian palazzo style by J Morant Lockyer – an authority on the Italian Renaissance period – and extended in 1916, when a stunning spiral staircase by Cecil Brewer was added. The beautiful bespoke chandelier from lighting specialists Bocci is a more recent addition (2013).

Offering 42,000ft^2 of retail space over three floors, Heal's is the ultimate destination for beautifully designed furniture, attractive modern decorations and cutting-edge kitchenware and lighting, featuring showrooms dedicated to top brands such as Kartell, Ligne Roset and Vitra, as well as in-store services such as bespoke furniture and interior design.

Heal's name is synonymous with quality and craftsmanship – its succinct motto is: 'Good Design. Well Made.' – and includes beds, rugs, fabrics and home accessories. Much more than simply a great place to shop, the store offers regular food tastings, demonstrations (from cake decorating to table setting) and a host of special events throughout the year. There's a lovely café, too.

Heal's, 196 Tottenham Court Rd, W1T 7LQ (020-7636 1666; www.heals.co.uk; Goodge St tube; Mon-Wed, Fri-Sat 10am-7pm, Thu 10am-8pm, Sun noon-6pm).

House of Hackney

Established in 2010 by husband and wife Javvy M Royle and Frieda Gormley, House of Hackney was first and foremost founded as a label, although its flagship store in Shoreditch has become a destination for fans of good design. Its aim was 'to take the beige out of interiors', with an emphasis on quality, design and English heritage. It has been an unqualified success and its products are available in over 65 partner stores worldwide, including Harrods and Liberty in London.

The award-winning House of Hackney store stocks all the brand's products, from eiderdowns and furniture to lampshades and wallpaper. There are echoes of William Morris around the store; both Javvy and Frieda are huge fans of the great British textile designer and social activist and share his values, and were approached in 2015 by the William Morris Gallery to re-imagine Morris for a new generation.

Since its inception, wherever possible House of Hackney has used small scale, skilled British manufacturers to bring its designs to life. Thus it has captured the zeitgeist with its British-made collection of prints and products: steeped in tradition but also bold and subversive for a truly modern statement.

House of Hackney, 131 Shoreditch High St, E1 6JE (020-7739 3901; www.houseofhackney.com; Shoreditch High St rail/Liverpool St tube; Mon-Sat 10am-7pm, Sun 11am-5pm).

Labour and Wait

Labour and Wait in trendy Shoreditch is housed in an old Truman Brewery pub and specialises in household goods: hardware, clothing, kitchenware, bathroom accessories, stationery and gifts. The concept may not sound exciting but the reality is fascinating. The store was established in 2000 by Rachel Wythe-Moran and Simon Watkins, who wanted to counter today's throwaway society where everything is expendable and only new and fashionable is worthwhile. They envisioned a place selling functional, well-designed, honest, timeless and aesthetically pleasing products to enhance everyday life.

Taking inspiration from Henry Wadsworth Longfellow's exhortation to 'learn to labour and to wait' (from his poem, *A Psalm of Life*), Wythe-Moran and Watkins have sourced products from specialist manufacturers around the world that fit their ethos, and in so doing have assembled a carefully curated collection of new and vintage items, some familiar, others waiting to be discovered; a collection of everyday classics that will mellow and improve with age.

Labour and Wait has a calm and ordered atmosphere and is a great place to browse. From a wall-mounted bottle opener to a flowerpot brush, it's packed with gems that you never knew you couldn't live without.

Labour & Wait, 85 Redchurch St, E2 7DJ (020-7729 6253; www.labourandwait.co.uk; Shoreditch High St rail; Tue-Sun 11am-6pm, closed Mon).

The Lighting Store

A family-run business founded in 1949, the Lighting Store is one of the last independent lighting retailers in London. Always at the cutting edge of lighting design,

fashion and technology, the store sources its products from around the world, including designs from Artemide, Foscarini and Flos, Swarovski chandeliers, LED fittings, handmade lampshades and fibre-optic lamps. It designs bespoke lighting for any setting from a mansion to a small flat, creating a light, bright, unique or intimate atmosphere. The Lighting Store also works with interior designers, developers and architects on commercial and residential projects.

The Lighting Store. 759-763 Finchley Rd, NW11 8DN (020-8731 8601; www.lightingstoredirect. co.uk; Golders Grn tube; Mon-Fri 9am-5.30pm, Sat 10am-5.30pm, closed Sun).

Little Paris

O pened in 2009, Little Paris in Crouch End is a Francophile's delight – a *mine de trésors* packed with an ever-changing eclectic mix of authentic, vintage and antique furniture, curiosities and accessories sourced from la belle France. From

contemporary French design items, such as whimsical jewellery and Parisian scarves and hats, to off-beat vintage homeware, the shop's two rooms are crammed with a mélange of crockery, vintage film posters, authentic Tolix chairs and Jieldé lamps.

Every few weeks Nicolas, the owner, hops over the Channel to visit his favourite ateliers, brocantes, dealers and markets, and returns with fresh treasures. While not cheap, prices are reasonable and most items are in excellent condition.

Little Paris, 39 Park Rd, N8 8TE (020-8340 9008; www.littleparis.co.uk; Highgate tube/Crouch Hill rail; Sun-Mon 11am-6pm, Tue-Sat 10am-6pm).

Lombok

Named after the idyllic Indonesian island, Lombok offers high quality, beautiful and uniquely designed Eastern-inspired furniture, lighting and accessories, handmade from natural materials and sourced with the good of the environment in mind. Though well-known for its Colonial-inspired dark teak furniture, Lombok's product range has grown to encompass different styles and finishes of wood, with hand finishing by skilled craftsmen imparting a personal feel. Proud of being an ethical producer, the company works closely with manufacturers in the Far East to ensure that the wood (reclaimed where possible) used in its products is sourced responsibly and legally.

Lombok, 204-208 Tottenham Court Rd, W1T 7PL (020-7637 3286; www.lombok.co.uk; Goodge St tube; Mon-Wed Fri-Sat 10am-7pm, Thu 10am-8pm, Sun noon-6pm).

Mint

Located in a quiet mews in South Kensington, Mint is a delightful interior design boutique offering an eclectic selection of cutting-edge contemporary pieces. Opened in 1998 by design consultant and interiors expert Lina Kanafani, Mint specialises in limited edition, exclusive and specially-commissioned furniture, glassware, textiles and ceramics from new and internationally-recognised designers. Looking more like an avant-garde design museum than a design shop, the white walls and pale flooring are flooded with light from the huge windows, which enhances the allure of the beautifully displayed works. Check out their spring and autumn exhibitions.

Mint also offers a comprehensive interior design consultation and furnishing service.

Mint, 2 North Ter, SW3 2BA (020-7225 2228; www.mintshop.co.uk; S Kensington tube; Mon-Wed, Fri-Sat 10:30am-6.30pm, Thu 10:30am-7.30pm, closed Sun).

Monologue

A ravishing new contemporary design-concept store in Shoreditch, Monologue was founded by interior designer Pavel Klimczack. With a focus on conceptual design with a Scandinavian slant, the store offers an exclusive selection of furniture, lighting, homeware, fashion accessories and stationery.

Its curated collection encompasses marble and bright pops of colour in an ever-evolving design space. Even if you can't afford to splash out several thousand pounds on a coffee table, it's still worth a visit – or a peek at the fabulous website – to see the gorgeous items on offer. If nothing else, Monologue offers a unique opportunity to discover the best of British and European contemporary talent.

Monologue, 93 Redchurch St, E2 7DP (07590-565884; www.monologuelondon.com; Shoreditch High St rail; Tue-Sat 10.30am-7pm, Sun 11am-6pm, closed Mon).

Pentreath & Hall

Founded by architect and designer Ben Pentreath in partnership with friend Bridie Hall, this delightful small shop in the heart of Bloomsbury

is a one-stop destination for home décor. It stocks well-designed and beautiful homeware including china, glass, linens, furniture, pictures, candles, vases, lights, antiques, books and more, sourced from throughout the UK, France, Belgium, Germany, Turkey and India, among other places. Pentreath & Hall is packed to the rafters with wonderful things not easily found elsewhere, from hand-blown glasses and colourful vases to stationery and art prints, kitchenware and lighting to cushions and candles. Utterly delightful.

Pentreath & Hall, 17 Rugby St, WC1N 3QT (020-7430 2526; www.pentreath-hall.com; Russell Sq tube; Mon-Sat 11am-6pm, closed Sun).

Pitfield London

A combination of homeware, design and lifestyle emporium, cool café and trendy art gallery, Pitfield epitomises the spirit of renewal and ingenuity in hip Hoxton. Occupying a huge double-fronted former office block with an edgy, industrial feel, it's the retail arm of celebrated interior designer Shaun Clarkson and business partner Paul Brewster, who have filled the bright, open-plan space with an eclectic assortment of pieces acquired at home and abroad.

Here you'll discover all manner of stylish furniture and home accessories, including colourful '70s seating, vintage glassware and lighting, exclusive Indian rugs, ultra-modern wallpaper from London designers, decorative objects, unique gifts and much more. The blend of old and new, budget-friendly and budget-busting – such as the inexpensive vintage coffee pots lined up alongside Reiko Kaneko's contemporary gold-accented teapots – gives the shop its distinctive character.

The café is an extension of the Pitfield lifestyle and a great place to work, relax and socialise, while tucking into freshly ground coffee with moreish meringues and brownies, delicious salads and tasty flatbreads. The exhibition space has played host to an array of new and established artists such as Jade Jagger, Louise West, Claire Brewster and James Brown, to name just a few.

Pitfield London, 31-35 Pitfield St, N1 6HB (020-7490 6852; http://pitfieldlondon.com; Old St tube/rail; daily 10am-7pm).

SCP East

Established in 1985 by Sheridan Coakley, SCP East is one of London's largest and best design stores, housed in a former furniture-manufacturing warehouse in hip Shoreditch (there's a second store,

SCP West, on Westbourne Grove). A much-loved part of the local community, it offers a unique blend of own-brand products, cutting-edge international design and 20th-century classics.

Spread across two floors, the store is a feast of design, whether you're looking to furnish your entire home or give it a lift with some special pieces. The first floor has larger items of furniture, lighting and rugs – and also houses an ever-evolving 'chair wall' – while the ground floor is given over to kitchenware, tableware, bathroom accessories, stationery, toys, technology, luggage and knitwear. It also has an area devoted to contemporary lighting and a broad selection of design books and magazines.

SCP's founding idea was to make and sell products that are functional, beautiful and made to last, and this remains its goal today. It employs many of the UK's best designers and is firmly established as one of Britain's most innovative and internationally respected manufacturers and suppliers of contemporary design.

SCP East, 135-139 Curtain Rd, EC2A 3BX (020-7739 1869; www.scp.co.uk; Old St tube/rail; Mon-Sat 9.30am-6pm, Sun 11am-5pm).

Skandium

A British company founded in 1999 by a Swede (Magnus Englund), a Finn (Christina Schmidt) and a Dane (Christopher Seidenfaden), Skandium's aim is to be 'the best retailer of Scandinavian design and furniture in the world'. It has four London stores, including the intriguingly named Republic of Fritz Hansen, but its flagship store (opened in 2007) is opposite the Brompton Oratory, housed in a building dating from the 1880s.

Skandium is the exclusive agent in the UK and Ireland for several Scandi brands, including Arabia and Höganäs ceramics, Hackman cookware, Iittala's classic and collectible 'objects', Room Copenhagan's Pantone mugs, Skagerak furniture and much more. It's a treasure house of design delights and not a flat-pack bookshelf in sight.

Skandium, 245-249 Brompton Rd, SW3 2EP (020-7584 2066; www.skandium.com; S Kensington tube; Mon-Wed, Fri-Sat 10am-6.30pm, Thu 10am-7pm, Sun 11am-5pm).

Squint

Established in 2005 in the living room of Lisa Whatmough, Squint is known for its exuberant patch-worked furniture, lighting, fabrics and wallpaper, all with more than a

touch of Willy Wonka about them. Through her passion for textiles and very British design sensibility, Lisa has created a world of richly decorative pieces that are a fusion of fashion and art.

All products are handmade, using top-quality materials, and include everything from cushions to chandeliers to a velvet-clad Chippendale desk. Squint designs are available through Harrods, Liberty, Conran, the Designers Guild and internationally, but the heart of the business is the Squint Studio in the Hackney Fashion Hub.

Squint, Studio 3, The Textile Building, 29A Chatham Pl, E9 6FJ (020-8986 6583; www. squintlimited.com; Hackney Central rail; Mon-Fri 10am-6pm, closed Sat-Sun).

Summerill & Bishop

Established in 1994 by June Summerill and Bernadette Bishop, this lovely kitchen shop has the allure of a Provençal home, filled with handcrafted earthenware, glassware and natural home products. The kitchen and tableware are a celebration of charming neutral, earthy tones, with vintage pieces alongside modern, simple and eclectic styles. Wares are sourced from the UK, Europe and further afield (including the Middle East and South Africa): many are handmade and hard to track down, such as a vintage double-bladed *hachoir* or hand-blown glass beads to suspend from your garden trees! Ranges include Astier de Villatte (tableware), Laguiole (knives) and Wonki Ware (ceramics).

Summerill & Bishop, 100 Portland Rd, W11 4LQ (020-7221 4566; www.summerillandbishop.com; Holland Pk tube; Mon-Sat 9am-6pm, closed Sun).

Thomas Goode

A London institution, Thomas Goode was founded in 1827 although its elegant Mayfair showroom, designed by Ernest George, dates from 1875. Holder of two royal warrants, Thomas Goode sells the world's finest tableware, from respected heritage brands to innovative contemporary designs. You can choose from fine English china, Meissen porcelain, glass and crystal-ware by Saint-Louis and Venini, and silverware and cutlery by Puiforcat, Odiot and Christofle. You can even have a bespoke dinner service made to your own specifications.

The showroom contains a museum dedicated to the company's rich design heritage, including two huge Minton elephants commissioned for the Paris Exhibition in 1889.

Thomas Goode & Co. Ltd, 19 S Audley St, W1K 2BN (020-7499 2823; www.thomasgoode.com; Green Pk tube; Mon-Sat 10am-6pm, closed Sun).

Tobias & the Angel

Starting life as a 'junk' shop in 1986, Tobias & the Angel (named after the owner, Angel Hughes, and a former partner) has evolved into a business best known for its block-printed fabrics and shades, custom-built furniture, accessories, and unique hand-made and vintage Christmas decorations. The furniture – hand-crafted in Surrey – is a sleek Scandinavian take on English country, including dressers, tables, chairs, drawer units, linen cupboards, desks, shelves and benches – painted in a choice of colours and priced per square foot! There's also a range of attractive accessories, including colourful cushions, delightful cat doorstops and unique lamps. T&A also provide an interior design service.

Tobias & the Angel, 68 White Hart Ln, SW13 0PZ (020-8878 8902; www.tobiasandtheangel.com; Barnes Br rail; Mon-Sat 10am-6pm, closed Sun).

Tom Dixon

A legend in his own lifetime, Tom Dixon is an award-winning, self-taught British designer (and former creative director of Habitat – see page 162), whose designs are sold in over 65 countries and have been acquired by museums across the globe. His canal-side store in west London showcases his contemporary and innovative furniture, lighting and homeware accessories, alongside an exclusive selection of pieces by approved design brands. From tables and chairs to mirrors and coat stands, the designs are inspired by Britain's unique heritage and explore the use of a wide range of materials and processes.

Tom Dixon, Wharf Building, Portobello Dock, 344 Ladbroke Gr, W10 5BU (020-7183 9737; www.tomdixon.net; Kensal Gn tube/rail; Mon-Sat 10am-6pm, Sun 11am-5pm).

Twentytwentyone

Established in 1996 on Islington's trendy Upper Street (now also with a showroom on River Street, EC1), Twentytwentyone are furniture and homeware retailers with a passion for iconic, original and vintage 20th-century design, which they sell alongside contemporary furniture, lighting and

accessories. They work with over 60 of the world's best designers and manufacturers, and their eclectic range includes pieces from Europe (particularly Scandinavia), the US, Japan and the Far East. Twentytwentyone's exciting and ever-changing range of designs is complimented by a broad cross-section of licensed reissues of classic designs from luminaries such as Aalto, Eames, Prouvé and Wegner.

Twentytwentyone, 274-275 Upper St, N1 2UA (020-7288 1996; http://twentytwentyone.com; Essex Rd rail/Angel tube; Mon-Sat 10am-6pm, Sun 11am-5pm).

The Water Monopoly

Founded by Justin Homewood in 1990, the Water Monopoly supplies some of the world's most beautiful bathrooms. Its 5,000ft^2 showroom in Queen's Park showcases both one-off originals (mostly French) and reproductions inspired by them. The constantly changing stock includes vintage copper tubs (prized for their original patina), ceramic basins, glamorous tri-fold mirrors, swan-neck taps and canopied shower units. These sit alongside UK-manufactured reproductions of fireclay tubs (in stone and resin) and cast iron baths made from recycled brake discs. If you can afford to splash out several thousand pounds on a bath, this is the place to do it.

Water Monopoly, 10-14 Lonsdale Rd, NW6 6RD (020-7624 2636; www.thewatermonopoly.com; Queen's Pk rail/Kilburn Pk tube; Mon-Thu 9am-6pm, Fri 9am-5pm, closed Sat-Sun).

Wawa

With a stellar reputation for creating fabulous furniture and accessories, Wawa was established by designer Richard Ward in 1998. The bespoke sofa collection is handmade to order in a converted Victorian warehouse in Shoreditch − a stone's throw from Columbia Road Flower Market (see page 207) − using the best of both modern and traditional materials and textiles. Richard's furniture includes

innovative solutions such as a sofa designed to fit into the angles of a Victorian bay window, a compact chaise longue which opens into a full-size double bed, and a rocking chair which folds virtually flat.

Wawa, 1 Ezra St, E2 7RH (020-7729 6768; www. wawa.co.uk; Hoxton rail; Mon-Fri, Sun 10am-6pm, closed Sat).

West Elm

Launched in Brooklyn (New York) in 2002, lifestyle store West Elm − from the same stable as US home furnishing giant Pottery Barn − opened its first UK outlet on Tottenham Court Road in 2013, just a few doors along from Habitat and Heal's. Anyone who has sampled the delights of American homeware stores will love this place, which is crammed with affordable understated New York chic − everything from cushions and cookware to bedding and furniture. West Elm is big on green credentials and is committed to ethical and sustainable production.

There's a Design Lab on the lower floor with an interior design service, plus an in-house café.

West Elm, 209 Tottenham Court Rd, W1T 7PN (020-7637 9150; www.westelm.co.uk; Goodge St tube; Mon-Wed, Fri-Sat 10am-7pm, Thu 10am-8pm, Sun noon-6pm).

Burlington Arcade

8.
Luxury Goods

As one of the world's great cities, home to a mammon of millionaires and billionaires, you would expect London to be awash with exclusive stores catering to expensive tastes. And indeed it is. From historic shops and exclusive boutiques to high-end department stores, the city has a wealth of vendors of luxury brands. This chapter features some of the best retailers (and manufacturers) of luxury goods, most of them British, including bespoke jewellers, designer watch boutiques, perfumers, silversmiths, and artisans making all manner of must-have goodies for the man or woman who has everything else.

Many of the stores featured are on Bond Street – one of the most expensive shopping streets in the world – but other popular destinations for big spenders include Jermyn Street in St James's, Savile Row and Burlington Arcade (the world's first shopping arcade). We've sourced the best places to buy jewellery, handbags, umbrellas and even bespoke mobile phones.

If you want to max out your credit card under one roof, London's famous department stores such as Harrods and Selfridges will be happy to help – the former offers 'All Things for All People, Everywhere' while the latter has a Wonder Room of exclusive brands.

Alfred Dunhill

The flagship branch of Alfred Dunhill – spread over three floors of Bourdon House, the only detached house in Mayfair and formerly the London residence of the Duke of Westminster – is more like an exclusive gentlemen's club than a menswear outlet. In addition to the usual suits, accessories, leather, aftershave and watches associated with the luxury brand, there's a spa and traditional barbers, a cellar bar (where customers can store their personal wine collection), restaurant and a 12-seat cinema room.

– made entirely by one artisan, whether for luggage or automotive interiors. Dunhill also offers a full grooming package, from manicures to massage, although it's the wet shaves and cuts that are most popular (you need to book weeks in advance). A spa area offers treatments for both men and women, while the Cellar bar does a great Bloody Mary or martini, which can be served at your barber's chair! A luxurious and uniquely British experience.

Alfred Dunhill, Bourdon House, 2 Davies St, W1K 3DJ (020-7385 8817; www.dunhill.com; Bond St tube; Mon-Sat 10am-7pm, closed Sun).

Alfred Dunhill built its reputation on its excellent menswear, particularly its made-to-measure suits and shirts, offering a choice of over 300 cloths for suits and 450 fabrics for shirts. The bespoke services also extend to handmade and embossed leather sets – reflecting the company's origin in saddlery

Aspinal of London

Established in 2001 by Iain Burton, Aspinal of London – with 11 London stores, including concessions in Harrods, House of Fraser and Selfridges – is a quintessential English luxury lifestyle brand, offering a wide range of exclusive leather goods and accessories. Its founding principle was to offer customers the most beautiful, elegant and refined designs of superior quality, and it never falls short of its goal.

In addition to ladies' handbags and men's bags, the company designs and manufactures a wide range of wallets and travel bags, as well as office and business goods such as briefcases. Aspinal also produces stationery products (diaries, journals, photo albums, etc.) and other items such as leather passport holders and travel accessories.

Invariably, these are beautiful objects of unsurpassed quality, with a British take on style, fusing classic functional designs with a quirky edge to create pieces for the modern man, woman and home. Its range of leather goods and bags are created by the company's own designers and handmade by craftspeople at their West Sussex headquarters. Aspinal is one of London's most exclusive gift emporiums, where almost everything can be monogrammed and service is second to none.

Aspinal of London, 46 Marylebone High St, W1U 5HQ (020-7224 0413; www.aspinaloflondon.com; Baker St tube; Mon-Wed, Fri-Sat 10am-6pm, Thu 10am-7pm, Sun 11am-5pm).

Asprey

Founded in 1781 by William Asprey as a silk printing business, Asprey soon evolved into a purveyor of luxury goods. It moved to its flagship store in New Bond Street in 1847 – the site was redeveloped in 2004 by Lord Foster – and grew to be one of the world's largest luxury goods stores. In 1990 Asprey merged with the jewellers Garrard (see page 185) but the two companies parted again in 2002.

Asprey is recognised as one of the UK's finest luxury-goods stores, famous for the manufacture and sale of jewellery, silverware, leather goods, timepieces, polo equipment and as a retailer of books. Its name is synonymous with refinement and luxury, and it has a long and distinguished relationship with British royalty dating back to the 1800s when Queen Victoria awarded the company its first royal

warrant; it has since held a royal warrant from every British monarch.

One thing that sets Asprey apart from its competitors is its on-site workshops. For much of its history these have been situated above its New Bond Street store (as they still are today). Here a team of innovative designers and craftsmen – including silversmiths, jewellers, leatherworkers, engravers and watchmakers – create the exquisite timeless treasures for which Asprey is world famous.

Asprey, 167 New Bond St, W1S 4AY (020-7493 6767; www.asprey.com; Green Pk tube; Mon-Sat 10am-6pm, closed Sun).

Bentley & Skinner

Royal jewellers Bentley & Skinner date back to 1880 and have been owned by the same families for three generations. Holding royal warrants for Her Majesty the Queen and His Royal Highness the Prince of Wales, this renowned jeweller specialises in buying and selling fine antique jewels, Fabergé and silver, and is noted for its unparalleled collection of engagement rings.

The company is also at the forefront of modern jewellery design and innovative goldsmithing techniques, and was responsible for such unique works as the Damien Hirst diamond skull, *For the Love of God* (pictured). Among the many services on offer are valuations for insurance and probate, repairs, pearl-stringing and bespoke jewellery commissions.

Bentley & Skinner, 55 Piccadilly, W1J 0DX (020-7629 0651; www.bentley-skinner.co.uk; Green Pk tube; Mon-Sat 10am-5.30pm, closed Sun).

Boodles

Founded in Liverpool in 1798 (as Boodle & Dunthorne) by the Wainwright family, Boodles is a privately-owned British jeweller and jewellery designer with stores in London, Liverpool, Manchester, Chester and Dublin. Its flagship London store on New Bond Street opened in 2007, with other outlets in Sloane Street, the Royal Exchange, Harrods and the Savoy Hotel.

A renowned silversmith, jeweller and watchmaker, in the 20th century Boodles designed and crafted many important trophies such as the solid gold cup awarded to the winner of the Grand National and awards for the Chelsea Flower Show. Since the '50s it has specialised in the acquisition of rare and exquisite gemstones, and in designing its own range of bespoke jewellery.

Boodles, 178 New Bond St, W1S 4RH (020-7437 5050; www.boodles.com; Green Pk tube; Mon-Sat 10am-6pm, closed Sun).

Burlington Arcade

The world's first shopping arcade running from Piccadilly to Burlington Gardens – and at almost 600 feet one of the longest covered shopping streets in the UK – Burlington Arcade opened to huge acclaim in 1819 and is today recognised as a historic and architectural masterpiece. It was built by Lord Cavendish to provide 'industrious females' with employment and to stop people throwing rubbish into the garden of Burlington House (which is adjacent to the arcade and now houses the Royal Academy of Arts). A haven of tranquillity and opulence, the arcade is home to purveyors of luxury goods and services: jewellery and watches, exquisite pens and leather goods, art and antiques, chocolates, perfumes and cashmere – there's even a traditional shoe-shine boy!

Entering the arcade from busy Piccadilly is like stepping back to the 19th century; the

red carpeted walkway, soft globe lights and dark wood shop fronts make shopping here a more genteel experience. Decorum is guarded by beadles in top hats and frockcoats – a private security force recruited from Lord Cavendish's 10th Hussars – who still patrol the arcade to this day, ensuring that no-one transgresses their rules which include no whistling, singing, humming, running, riding bicycles, opening umbrellas or behaving boisterously in the arcade.

Burlington Arcade, 51 Piccadilly, W1J 0QJ (020-7493 1764; www.burlington-arcade.co.uk; Green Pk tube; Mon-Sat 9am-7.30pm, Sun 11am-6pm).

David Morris

B espoke jeweller David Morris was established in 1962 and shot to fame a year later when Morris and his design partner were awarded the 9th De Beers Diamonds International Award in New York (they won it again in 1964). Now firmly established as one of London's (and the world's) most esteemed jewellery brands, the enviable client list includes Queen Noor of Jordan, 'Queen' of Hollywood Elizabeth Taylor, Princess Margaret, Princess Anne and Diana, Princess of Wales.

The company is now managed by David's son, Jeremy, who is also the principal designer, and continues to design and craft dazzling couture jewellery to the very highest standards.

David Morris, 180 New Bond St, W1S 4RL (020-7499 2200; www.davidmorris.com; Green Pk tube; Mon-Fri 10am-6pm, Sat 10.30am-5pm, closed Sun).

De Beers

F ounded in 1888 by the legendary Cecil Rhodes – British imperialist, mining magnate, politician and founder of the African territory of Rhodesia – De Beers has been the pre-eminent name in diamonds for over 125 years. Majority owned by the Oppenheimer family for 80 years until 2011 (when it sold its stake to Anglo American), De Beers is famous for the phrase 'A Diamond Is Forever', considered among the best advertising slogans of the 20th century.

Today the company is one of the world's principal creators of exquisite diamond jewellery, through the selection of the world's finest diamonds, impeccable craftsmanship and sophisticated designs.

De Beers, 50 Old Bond St, W1S 4QT (020-7758 9700; www.debeers.co.uk; Bond St tube; Mon-Sat 10am-6pm, closed Sun).

Department Stores

If there's one thing London's department stores (see **Chapter 4**) – particularly Fortnum & Mason, Harrods, Harvey Nichols, Liberty and Selfridges – are noted for, it's the wide range of luxury goods they offer, including exclusive items unavailable elsewhere. If you want to splash the cash and money is no object, you can do no better than visit Harrods in Knightsbridge – offering seven floors of luxury products from the world's foremost brands – where you can buy anything from the proverbial silver spoon to a gold-plated Rolls-Royce! They even have a real estate department and you can charter an Air Harrods helicopter to view properties…

London's major department stores offer everything from fine jewellery and designer watches – all the best names under one roof – to haute couture and fashion accessories, luxury perfumes and exclusive handbags to exquisite writing implements and personalised stationery, delectable food and wine to beautiful antiques, fine art and a plethora of lavish gifts. All department stores offer a gift service, particularly for weddings, while Harrods have an exclusive gift concierge service. Other services include travel planning, theatre tickets, interpreters and gift wrapping.

And if you need help emptying your purse or wallet, most stores offer a personal shopping service, with experts on hand to offer independent advice and inspiration.

See Chapter 4 for addresses and contact details.

Floris

Begun in 1730 by Juan Famenias Floris (originally from Menorca), Floris is the oldest independent family-owned perfumer in the world and still occupies its original premises. It's the only appointed perfumer to Her Majesty the Queen and was granted its first royal warrant by George IV in 1820 – which was followed by 19 others.

Its wide range of products are still developed in Jermyn Street by the in-house perfumer team and are approved by Edward Bodenham, the Floris 'nose' and a 9th-generation member of the Floris family. Floris also creates bespoke perfumes, giving customers the opportunity to customise an existing Floris scent.

Floris, 89 Jermyn St, SW1Y 6JH (020-7747 3612; www.florislondon.com; Piccadilly Circus tube; Mon-Wed, Fri 9.30am-6.30pm, Thu 9.30am-7pm, Sat 10am-7pm, Sun 11.30am-5.30pm).

Garrard

Garrard is the oldest jewellery house in the world, founded in 1735 by George Wickes (1698-1761), when records show it received a royal commission from Frederick, Prince of Wales. More recently it made the sapphire engagement ring (pictured) given by Prince William, Duke of Cambridge, to his wife Catherine – and previously worn by his mother, the late Princess Diana. The company also has a long history of making sporting trophies, including sailing's America's Cup.

Noted for its timeless design, Garrard has a reputation for its superb craftsmanship and utmost attention to detail, specialising in the design and manufacture of (in its own words) 'magnificent jewellery today, to become the heirlooms of tomorrow'.

Garrard, 24 Albemarle St, W1S 4HT (020-7518 1070; http://garrard.com; Green Pk tube; Mon-Fri 10am-6pm, Sat 10am-5pm, closed Sun).

General Eyewear

Established in the late '90s by Fraser Laing, General Eyewear is a frame workshop and eyewear boutique based in Camden Town. It's one of London's leading designers of bespoke eyewear, creating personalised frames to order – clients consult with an eyewear stylist and a frame designer in order to obtain a design that's pleasing, elegant and appropriate. General Eyewear also provides a full range of optical services (but no eye tests!).

GE's vast design resource consists of historical frames, sunglasses, goggles and visors, as well as production prototypes, catalogues and custom-made catwalk pieces which are often used in collaborations with international film and fashion companies.

General Eyewear, Arch 67, The Stables Market, Camden Market, Chalk Farm Rd, NW1 8AH (020-7428 0123; www.generaleyewear.com; Camden Town tube; daily 10am-6pm).

Geo F Trumper

A traditional gentleman's barber and perfumer, Geo F Trumper still operates from its original store in Curzon Street, Mayfair (there's a second branch in Duke of York Street, W1), where it was established by George Trumper in the 19th century. The shop still contains the original mahogany cubicles and glass display cases, although nowadays it's air-conditioned for clients' comfort.

Trumper's services include haircutting, shaving, tinting, moustache and beard trimming, manicure and pedicure, facial cleansing and massage. It also markets its own range of shaving equipment, skin-care products, aftershave and colognes, along with cufflinks, ties, umbrellas, canes and leather goods. Pure pampering for men about town.

Geo F Trumper, 9 Curzon St, W1J 5HQ (020-7499 1850; www.trumpers.com; Green Pk tube; Mon-Fri 9am-5.30pm, Sat 9am-5pm, closed Sun).

Graff

Founded in London in 1960 by Laurence Graff – a poor boy from London's East End now dubbed the 'King of Bling' – Graff Diamonds now has some 35 stores in cities around the world, including New York, Monte Carlo, Geneva, Tokyo, Beijing, Hong Kong, Paris and San Francisco. The company's operations comprise the design, manufacture and retail distribution of high-end jewellery and watches, with sales reaching a record US$1billion in 2014, buoyed by demand from the Middle and Far East.

Graff has handled more diamonds of notable rarity and beauty than any other jeweller, ranging from centuries-old stones to newly discovered gems. One famous example of its work is the Peacock Brooch (pictured), taking the form of a peacock with a display of fanned tail feathers; the diamond brooch features a collection of coloured diamonds totalling over 120 carats – with a rare 20-carat deep blue pear-shaped diamond at its centre – and is valued at $100 million.

Graff has been the victim of a number of robberies, including the largest ever gems heist in the UK in 2009, when jewellery worth nearly £40 million was stolen from the New Bond Street store. None of it was ever recovered.

Graff, 6-8 New Bond St, W1S 3SJ (020-7584 8571; www.graffdiamonds.com; Green Pk tube; Mon-Fri 9am-6pm, Sat 10am-5pm, closed Sun).

Hatton Garden

The centre of London's jewellery trade since medieval times, Hatton Garden – named after Sir Christopher Hatton (1540-1591, pictured), a favourite of Elizabeth I

who became Lord Chancellor in 1587 – is both the name of a street and an area on the fringe of the City of London, bordered by Clerkenwell Road, Gray's Inn Road, Holborn and Farringdon Road. It has an international reputation as the centre of London's diamond trade and is one of the world's finest luxury jewellery centres. De Beers (see page 183) has its UK HQ here and Laurence Graff (see page 187) opened his first jewellery store here in 1962.

With some 300 businesses and over 50 shops, Hatton Garden contains the largest and most concentrated cluster of jewellery retailers in the UK, employing over 1,000 of Britain's finest jewellers, craftspeople and designers. The quarter offers generations of expertise in a wide choice of styles, from antique and classic through to contemporary and futurist.

Not surprisingly, it's also of great interest to criminals. In April 2015, jewellery and valuables valued at some £200 million were stolen by a team of elderly thieves from an underground safe deposit in Hatton Garden in the 'largest burglary in English legal history'.

Hatton Garden, EC1 (www.hatton-garden. net; Farringdon/Chancery Ln tube; Mon-Sun, although not all stores are open at weekends).

Mappin & Webb

From Jonathan Mappin's small cutlery workshop, established in 1775 in Sheffield to create beautifully crafted silverware, Mappin & Webb has grown to become one of the most iconic names in English jewellery. The company is internationally renowned for its classic silverware, elegant fine jewellery collections and luxury timepieces from some of the most prestigious Swiss watch houses, including Jaeger-LeCoultre, Patek Philippe and Rolex.

Mappin & Web has a long association with royalty (it currently holds two royal warrants), which was further cemented in 2012 by the appointment of Mappin & Webb's master craftsman to the position of Crown Jeweller (custodian of the Crown Jewels) .

Mappin & Webb, 1 Old Bond St, W1S 4PB (020-7499 1331; www.mappinandwebb.com; Green Pk tube; Mon-Wed, Fri-Sat 10am-6pm, Thu 10am-7pm, Sun noon-5pm).

Marcus Watches

The origins of Marcus Watches date back to 1932, when Alexander Margulies (a Polish immigrant) set up business as a clock and watch salesman. He established Time Products, which today owns the Marcus and Hublot fine watch stores on Bond Street as well as Sekonda, the UK's best-selling watch brand.

His son Marcus joined the company in 1963 and has established Marcus Watches as one of the principal 'haute horology' retailers in the world, specialising in complications and tourbillons (the most sophisticated precision timepieces). The New Bond Street boutique is a prime destination for watch lovers, with many rare and unique masterpieces including one of the world's largest collections by renowned Swiss watchmaker Audemars Piguet.

Marcus Watches, 170 New Bond St, W1S 4RB (020-7290 6500; www.marcuswatches.com; Green Pk tube; Mon-Sat 10.30am-5.30pm, closed Sun).

E. B. Meyrowitz

One of the UK's leading designers of handmade spectacles, Emil Bruno Meyrowitz was born in 1852 in Greifenhagen, Prussia. He was a pioneer in optics, with practices in London, Paris and New York, and designed his own line of optical and medical products for a distinguished international clientele.

Today Meyrowitz continues to design spectacles and sunglasses – mostly manufactured in the UK – exclusively for its boutique, created from the finest acetate, buffalo horn and other rare materials. Most are made-to-measure to a client's exact specifications, combining different styles, colours and materials to create a bespoke product. A shop with unique specs appeal!

E. B. Meyrowitz, 6 The Royal Arcade, 28 Old Bond St, W1S 4SF (020-7493 5778; www. ebmeyrowitz.co.uk; Bond St tube; Mon-Wed, Fri 10am-6pm, Thu 10am-7pm, Sat 10am-5.30pm, closed Sun).

Miller Harris

Lyn Harris spent five years training in Paris and Grasse (at Robertet, the world's leader in natural aromatic ingredients, with whom she still collaborates) and created bespoke fragrances for private clients before founding Miller Harris (named after her father) in 2000. The company specialises in luxury fragrances and bespoke perfumes, combining Parisian elegance with London's eclectic street styles.

In addition to the 20 or so fine perfumes and bath and body products sold in her elegant boutiques in Mayfair – the Bruton Street shop is heavy on black lacquer –

and Covent Garden, MH also concocts in-house fragrances for Liberty and jeweller Solange Azagury-Partridge.

Miller Harris, 21 Bruton St, W1J 6QD (020-7629 7750; www.millerharris.com; Green Pk tube; Mon-Wed, Fri-Sat 10am-6pm, Thu 10am-7pm, closed Sun).

Moussaieff

One of the world's most exclusive and discreet fine jewellers, Moussaieff is a family business dating back to the mid-19th century when its founder traded pearls in the Persian Gulf.

It's now run by Alisa Moussaieff who, with over 55 years' experience, is one of the most influential and respected players in the diamond market, known for her instinct and passion for rare and incomparable gems.

Moussaieff's glamorous creations attract a prestigious international clientele, from royalty and celebrities to collectors and connoisseurs. Flamboyant designs coupled with exceptional craftsmanship from their Paris workshops create exquisite jewellery which is an investment as well as an adornment. Prices are beyond most pockets – but anyone can browse.

Moussaieff, 172 New Bond St, W1S 4RE (020-7290 1536; www.moussaieff.co.uk; Green Pk tube; Mon-Fri 10am-6pm, Sat 10.30am-5.30pm, closed Sun).

Mulberry

There are Mulberry stores all over London but perhaps the most exclusive is the one in New Bond Street, where you can bag goodies from one of Britain's most famous lifestyle brands. Noted for its leather poacher bags, Mulberry was founded in 1971 by Roger Saul; former creative director Emma Hill (who joined in 2007) is credited with turning the company from a trusted briefcase and wallet maker into an international fashion powerhouse, beloved by celebrities including the Duchess of Cambridge.

Today the range includes male and female fashion, leather goods and accessories – notably handbags – and footwear. Mulberry continues to make designer leather goods at its original

Somerset factory, although many products are now made overseas.

Mulberry, 50 New Bond St, W1S 1BJ (020-7491 3900; www.mulberry.com; Bond St tube; Mon-Sat 10am-7pm, Sun noon-6pm).

Ormonde Jayne

Launched in 2001 by self-taught 'nose' Linda Pilkington, Ormonde Jayne is a luxury perfume company selling beautiful original perfumes, scented candles and bath oils. All products – which bear exotic names

such as Orris Noir (based on the Black Iris flower) and Tiare (featuring Tahiti's national flower) – are created by Linda, and packaged by hand in her London workshop.

She opened her sumptuous bijou shop – with antique gold wall coverings and black glass chandeliers – in the Royal Arcade in 2006, and has an enviable celebrity clientele list including Elton John, Will Smith and Bryan Ferry, while Anouska Hempel places OJ's grapefruit candles in her five-star hotels.

Ormonde Jayne, 12 Royal Arcade, 28 Old Bond St, W1S 4SL (020-7499 1100; www.ormondejayne. com; Green Pk tube; Mon-Sat 10am-6pm, closed Sun).

Penfriend

Founded in 1950 by Ivan Mason, a former Parker mechanic, Penfriend sells vintage and contemporary pens, and is the world's largest independent pen restorer. The shop stocks over 1,000 fountain pens, ballpoints and pencils from makers such as Parker – including a wide range of Parker 51s and 61s, in both standard and rare colours, as well as 9 and 18 carat gold models – Waterman, Mont Blanc, Cross, Pelikan, Montegrappa, Graf Von Faber Castell, Caran D'ache, Yard-O-Led and Lamy.

Penfriend also stocks a huge selection of nibs (italic, oblique, flexible, etc.) and writing accessories such as colourful inks, refills, blotters, pen pouches and quills. There's a second branch on Fleet Street.

Penfriend, 34 Burlington Arcade, W1J 0QA (020-7499 6337; www.penfriend.co.uk; Green Pk tube; Mon-Fri 9.30am-5.30pm, Sat 10am-6pm, closed Sun).

Penhaligon's

This world-renowned perfumer began life as a barber's shop in 1870. William Penhaligon offered his first gentlemen's fragrance in 1872 – Hammam Bouquet, inspired by the steam and sulphurous aromas from a neighbouring Turkish Bath!

It's still sold today, as is the best-selling Blenheim Bouquet, created in 1902 for the Duke of Marlborough;

with its zesty citrus, spices and woods, it broke with the prevailing floral trends of its day. Ladies' classics include the timeless and beguiling Bluebell.

Today Penhaligon's has a portfolio of some 38 unusual and distinctive fragrances that are continually being added to. The immaculate Wellington Street boutique (there's another in the Covent Garden Market Building) also contains a small museum.

Penhaligon's, 41 Wellington St, WC2E 7BN (020-7240 6256; www.penhaligons.com; Covent Gdn tube, Mon-Wed 10am-6pm, Thu-Sat 10am-7pm, Sun noon-6pm).

Pickett

Started in 1988 by Trevor Pickett – the quintessential English eccentric – Pickett sells exclusive handmade leather goods and accessories, from bags (handbags, luggage, briefcases, etc.) to chess sets and photo frames. It has expanded from traditional men's leather wallets and belts to include contemporary products such as leather iPhone covers, and also stocks exquisite Kilim slippers (made from offcuts of authentic Turkish flat-weave rugs) and luxuriously soft pashminas.

The company takes great pride in its unique range of products, manufactured by small specialist workshops and craftspeople, some of whom have worked with Pickett for over 25 years. There's also a bespoke service for everything from leather goods to jewellery.

Pickett, 10-12 Burlington Gdns, W1S 3EY (020-7493 8939; www.pickett.co.uk; Piccadilly Circus tube; Mon-Wed, Fri 9.30am-6.30pm; Thu 10am-7pm, Sat 10am-6pm, Sun noon-6pm).

Searle

Established in the City in 1893, Searle & Co is one of London's premier silversmiths, specialising in antique and modern jewellery, and antique (especially fine Georgian and Victorian items), contemporary and reproduction silverware. Searle is at the forefront of the design, manufacture and sale of high quality bespoke silverware and jewellery to commemorate special occasions such as weddings, anniversaries, engagements, christenings and birthdays. Other services include seal and general engraving, repairs, restoration and appraisals.

Although fashions and trends have changed considerably over the past 120 years, Searle's commitment to producing silverware and jewellery of the highest quality has remained constant.

Searle, 1 Royal Exchange, EC3V 3LL (020-7626 2456; www.searleandco.ltd.uk; Bank tube; Mon-Fri 9.30am-5pm, closed Sat-Sun).

Smythson

Frank Smythson was an ardent enthusiast of meticulous craftsmanship and exceptional quality when he set up shop in Bond Street in 1887. Today his company has over 125 years' experience of creating luxury leather goods – handbags, travel goods, business accessories and personal stationery – and has a reputation for superb quality, functionality and exquisite craftsmanship.

Smythson has long catered to the rich and famous, from European royalty to Hollywood legends and movers and shakers of the 20th century, boasting Grace Kelly, Vivien Leigh, Sigmund Freud and Sir Winston Churchill among its illustrious past clients. The company also holds three current royal warrants.

Smythson, 40 New Bond St, W1S 2DE (020-7629 8558; www.smythson.com; Bond St tube; Mon-Wed, Fri 9.30am-7pm, Thu 10am-8pm, Sat 10am-7pm, Sun noon-6pm).

Swaine Adeney Brigg

One of Britain's oldest and most prestigious manufacturers of leather goods and umbrellas, Swaine Adeney Brigg was founded in 1750 when John Ross established a whip-making business at 238 Piccadilly. James Swaine purchased the business in 1798 and Brigg was added when umbrella-makers Thomas Brigg & Sons (est. 1838) merged with Swaine Adeney in 1943. The group also

incorporates Papworth Travel Goods, acquired in 1997, and the hatters Herbert Johnson (est. 1872), makers of military hats and exclusive fur felt hats and tweed caps.

The SAB range of handmade umbrellas and leather goods – which includes attachés, holdalls, trunks, suitcases, folios, and document and computer cases, to name just a few – are hand-made in England in time-honoured tradition using bridle leather

and brass hardware. It has involved into a luxury lifestyle brand beloved by business travellers, royalty (it holds a number of royal warrants and supplied the whips for the carriages at the wedding of Prince William and Kate Middleton) and Hollywood heroes. SAB made the original Bond attaché case for the 1963 film *From Russia with Love* and also provided the Herbert Johnson 'poet' hat worn by Indiana Jones (Harrison Ford) in the film *Raiders of the Lost Ark*.

Swaine Adeney Brigg, 7 Piccadilly Arcade, Jermyn St, SW1Y 6NH (020-7409 7277; www. swaineadeneybrigg.com; Mon-Fri 9.30am-6pm, Sat 10am-5.30pm, closed Sun).

Theo Fennell

The head of one of Britain's best known jewellery and silverware companies, Theo Fennell began his career as an apprentice at heritage silversmith Edward Barnard in Hatton Garden, before launching his own company in 1982. Today his one-off

pieces are designed and made by his in-house team in workshops above the Fulham Road flagship store.

Theo Fennell jewellery collections range from the classically discreet to the unashamedly sexy, from sleek minimalism to breath-taking complexity. The witty, original designs are instantly recognisable, from elegant modern pieces to the theatrical stunners that make headlines. The style is inspired by the ancient and classic as well

as the new and revolutionary, using both traditional skills and cutting-edge techniques.

Theo makes many bespoke one-off pieces of jewellery, both commissions and on a whim, which are all original. His silverware is both practical and beautiful – from coffee pots

to jam jar tops – and is regularly commissioned by private individuals and corporate clients. He also designs trophies, including one for the Italian Formula One Grand Prix, and has exhibited at the Royal Academy.

Theo Fennell, 169 Fulham Rd, SW3 6SP (020-7591 5000; www.theofennell.com; S Kensington tube; Mon-Sat 10am-6pm, closed Sun).

Vertu

Established by Finnish mobile-phone manufacturer Nokia in 1998, Vertu is a British manufacturer and retailer of luxury handmade mobile phones. Vertu phones are a unique blend of superb craftsmanship, superior performance and personal concierge services; the latter includes 24-hour worldwide assistance, recommendations and priority bookings (similar to the services offered by exclusive credit cards).

Each phone is handmade by a single craftsperson at the company's factory in England using exceptional materials such as titanium, gold and gemstones, each selected not just for their beauty but also for their exceptional strength. Now you can ring with bling – every billionaire should have at least one!

Vertu, 38 Old Bond St, W1S 4QW (020-3205 1123; www.vertu.com/gb/en; Green Pk tube; Mon-Sat 10am-6pm, closed Sun).

Watches & Jewellery of Bond Street

Owned by Raj Jain, Watches & Jewellery of Bond Street is one of London's premier dealers in vintage and pre-owned watches and jewellery. The company has been dealing in rare and vintage watches such as Audemars Piguet, Cartier, Patek Philippe and Vacheron & Constantin internationally since 1990. The authenticity of each watch is guaranteed; they come with a warranty and the company offers a buy-back or part exchange facility, in addition to repairs and servicing.

W&J are also a leading retailer of pre-owned luxury jewellery brands including Bulgari, Boucheron, Cartier, Chaumet, Fabergé, Gucci, Hermès, Tiffany and many more. But there's nothing secondhand about the sparkle…

Watches & Jewellery of Bond Street, 74 New Bond St, W1S 1RT (020-7491 0042; www. watchcentre.com and www.richdiamonds.com; Bond St tube; Mon-Fri 10am-5.30pm, Sat 11am-5.30pm, closed Sun).

Apple Market, Covent Garden

9.
Markets

Energetic, eclectic and always entertaining, London's markets portray the city's commerce at its most colourful, and are great hunting grounds for shrewd shoppers looking for a bargain. They offer everything from antiques, clothes and curios to food, flowers and homeware, and come in all shapes and sizes, from vast, sprawling iconic markets such as Borough, Camden and Portobello, to local community and farmers' markets. This chapter features around 30 of the city's best, from specialist trade markets like Billingsgate and Smithfield to tiny artisan foodie markets; from collectors' markets such as Greenwich to ethnic markets like Whitechapel and those specialising in delicious street food.

Independent traders and passionate local communities are at the heart of London's market scene, where you'll encounter many budding entrepreneurs, particularly when it comes to food. Produce ranges from the exotic to artisan and caters for all tastes – a delectable bounty of variety and colour. You can shop for every conceivable ingredient and snack your way around the world; indeed, there's no more pleasurable way to shop than stall-hopping at one of these foodie festivals.

See also the Southbank Centre Book Market (page 50) and **Chapter 1** for antiques markets.

Billingsgate Market

Situated in East London, Billingsgate Fish Market is the UK's largest inland fish market, taking its name from Billingsgate – originally known as Blynesgate and Byllynsgate – in the City of London, where the riverside market was originally located. The market rights of the City of London were based in a charter granted by Edward III in 1327, although Billingsgate didn't become formally established until an Act of Parliament in 1699.

Roget Barton, market trader

In 1982 the Market was relocated to a new 13-acre (5.3ha) complex close to Canary Wharf in Docklands. Most of the fish sold through the market now arrives by road, from ports as far afield as Aberdeen and Cornwall, although live imports include lobsters from Canada and eels from New Zealand. The ground floor of the building consists of a large trading hall with around 100 stands and 30 shops, including two cafés. Some 25,000 tonnes of fish and fish products are sold annually at Billingsgate (around 40 per cent imported from abroad), which has an annual turnover of some £200 million.

Billingsgate is open to the general public and is an interesting place to visit, although if you're buying fish you need to arrive early (it opens at 4am) for the best choice. There's also an excellent Seafood (cookery) School – see www.seafoodtraining.org.

Billingsgate Market, Trafalgar Way, E14 5ST (020-7987 1118; www.cityoflondon.gov.uk/business/wholesale-food-markets/billingsgate; Poplar DLR; Tue-Sat 4-9.30am, closed Sun-Mon).

Borough Market

Borough Market in Southwark was first recorded in 1276, although some claim a market has existed in the area since the 11th century and possibly much earlier. Despite changing locations a number of times, and even being temporarily abolished in the 18th century, the market has thrived and today is the largest wholesale and retail artisan food market in London, selling a huge variety of produce sourced from throughout Britain and around the globe. It's run by a charitable trust and is the only fully independent market in London.

Since its renaissance as a retail market in the early 21st century – it still operates as a wholesale market from 2-8am on weekdays – Borough Market has become a mecca for those who care about the quality and provenance of the food they cook, sell or eat, including chefs, restaurateurs, gourmets, foodies and keen amateur cooks.

It seems that anyone who's anyone in London's artisan food world has an outlet at Borough Market, including Artisan du Chocolat, Ginger Pig (see page 134), Konditor & Cook, Monmouth Coffee and Neal's Yard Dairy (see page 143). If anywhere in the capital illustrates Britain's newfound love of good food, it's Borough Market.

Borough Market, 8 Southwark St, SE1 1TL (020-7407 1002; www.boroughmarket.org.uk; London Br rail/tube; limited market, Mon-Tue 10am-5pm; full market, Wed-Thu 10am-5pm, Fri 10am-6pm, Sat 8am-5pm, closed Sun).

Brick Lane Market

Brick Lane in Tower Hamlets got its name in the 15th century when it was the home of London's brick and tile manufacturers, although it later became a centre for the brewing industry. Today, it's an artistic multicultural melting pot, and its weekend markets attract hordes of (mostly young) people in search of secondhand furniture, household goods, records and CDs, cheap antiques, vintage clothing, jewellery, arts and crafts, books, general bric-a-brac and food.

Dating back to the 18th century, the market is pure East End, chaotic and haphazard – somewhere between a treasure trove and a junk heap – with a surprise around every corner. The joy is that you never know what you'll find; anything from cheap leather and vintage clothes to old magazines and kitsch collectibles, stunning silks to period furniture. Go on a Sunday to catch it at its best, when the

Sunday Upmarket in Ely's Yard (in the Old Truman Brewery) houses over 200 stalls selling fashion, accessories, crafts, interiors and music, along with a large indoor food area offering a wealth of local and ethnic delights.

Brick Lane Market, The Old Truman Brewery, 146 Brick Ln, E1 6RU (020-7770 6028; www. backyardmarket.co.uk, www.boilerhouse-foodhall.co.uk, www.sundayupmarket.co.uk, www.visitbricklane.org; Aldgate E or Shoreditch High St tube; Sat 11am-6pm, Sun 10am-5pm).

Brixton Market

Brixton Market is actually a number of markets thrown together in a gloriously haphazard manner. It comprises a vibrant street market and three elegant covered

arcades: Reliance Arcade, Market Row and Granville Arcade (now collectively rebranded Brixton Village and packed with culinary treats) which are open daily. A more recent addition is Brixton Station Road, hosting both a food market on Fridays and a Sunday farmers' market.

After a huge wave of immigration in the '50s, the market became an important focal point for the black community. It sells a wide range of foods and goods, but is best known for its African and Caribbean produce, including specialities such as flying fish, breadfruit and all manner of weird-looking meats, reflecting the diverse community of Brixton and the surrounding areas.

The market has a heaving, bustling atmosphere that you won't find elsewhere in London; whereas many markets are interesting to browse and attract tourists as much as shoppers, Brixton Market is a 'real' market selling a wide choice of world produce at affordable prices with minimum frills. The Atlantic Road part of the market offers more in the way of clothes, leather goods, household linen and children's toys.

Brixton Market, Electric Ave, Pope's Rd and Brixton Station Rd, SW9 (020-7926 2530; http://brixtonmarket.net; Brixton tube; see website for times).

Broadway & Netil Markets

Spend Saturday at Broadway and Netil Markets in East London, where Broadway Market – running from London Fields south to Regent's Canal – has been welcoming shoppers since the 1890s. A

Saturday food market was launched in 2004 and now boasts over 100 stalls selling artisan foods, street food and drinks, while cafés, restaurants, pubs and myriad independent shops line the streets. The market is also popular for its vintage and designer togs, bric-a-brac, books, flowers and crafts.

Neighbouring Netil Market – an altogether more sedate affair – is located on Westgate Street, where you'll find additional food stalls plus vintage homeware, jewellery designers, illustrators, original artwork, vintage clothing, accessories and more.

Broadway Market, E8 (www.broadwaymarket. co.uk; London Fields rail; Sat 9am-5pm) and Netil Market, 13-23 Westgate St, E8 3RL (http:// netilmarket.tumblr.com; Sat 11am-6pm).

Cabbages & Frocks

The delightfully named Cabbages & Frocks market is held every Saturday in the cobbled yard of St Marylebone Parish Church off Marylebone High Street in Marylebone Village. It's one of London's loveliest neighbourhoods with a wealth of interesting independent shops, cafés and restaurants. Here you can buy delicious artisan and organic foods – olive oil, balsamic syrup and vinegar, divine cupcakes, fine bread, olives, cheese, Argentinian steak sandwiches, hog roast, Japanese delicacies, hot chocolate, organic crepes and galettes, and more – plus handicrafts from local designers and cottage industries, including retro and vintage clothing (and children's clothes), homeware, hand-blown glass and jewellery.

Cabbages & Frocks Market, St Marylebone Parish Church Grounds, Marylebone High St, W1U 5BA (020-7794 1636; www. cabbagesandfrocks.co.uk; Baker St tube; Sat 11am-5pm).

Camden Market

Created as an arts and crafts market in the '70s, Camden Market (or markets) is one of the city's coolest destinations for trendy Londoners and visitors. The market is comprised of six adjoining markets in Camden Town near Camden Lock (also called Hampstead Road Lock) on Regent's Canal, collectively called 'Camden Market' or 'Camden Lock'. People flock here to buy an eclectic jumble of bric-a-brac, antiques and collectibles, retro and vintage fashion, ethnic art, rugs and kilims, jewellery, furniture, music and food (especially street food). One of London's largest and most popular markets, it's best at weekends when it attracts up to 150,000 bargain hunters.

Camden Lock Market, established in 1974, was the original craft market but now offers a much wider range of goods, while the ever popular Camden Stables Market is the centre of the alternative fashion scene.

The market is the creative and cultural heart of London, featuring some of the city's best designers, artists and independent vendors, as well as great food and drink. The West Yard hosts the Global Kitchen – which wafts its heady aroma of spices across the canal-side terraces – home to some of the city's most exciting street-food vendors.

Camden Lock Market, Chalk Farm Rd, NW1 8AF (020-3763 9999; www.camdenmarket.com, www.camdenlock.net and www.camdenlockmarket.com; Chalk Farm/Camden Town tube; daily 10am-6pm).

Chapel Market

A traditional street market (daily except Mondays), Chapel Market is situated near the Angel in Islington. It consists of 150-200 stalls selling fresh fruit and veg, meat and fish, household and electrical goods, cheap clothes and footwear, flowers and plants, travel goods and accessories, jewellery and watches, and cards and stationery, as well as street-food stalls and services such as key cutting and knife sharpening. In addition to the market stalls, interesting small boutiques, shops and chain stores line the street. On Sundays the market incorporates Islington Farmers' Market − the city's first farmers' market − between Baron Street and Penton Street.

Chapel Market, Chapel St, N1 9EX (Angel tube; Tue-Sat 9am-6pm; Sun 8.30am-4pm, closed Mon).

Church Street Market

Starting as a hay market in 1830, nowadays Church Street Market is an authentic unglamorous street market in the best London tradition. A unpretentious community-oriented market with a multicultural flavour, it hosts between 50 and 150 stalls offering cheap clothing and accessories, bargain household goods, jewellery, luggage, leather goods, fish, meat, fruit and vegetables (great value), and street food.

Bell Street, which runs parallel to Church Street, has a separate market on Fridays and Saturdays offering cheap secondhand clothes, records and electrical goods. At the eastern end of Church Street (near Lisson Grove) you'll find Alfies Antique Market (see page 10) and a cluster of antique shops.

Church Street Market, Church St, NW8 8DT (Marylebone tube; Mon-Sat 8am-6pm, closed Sun).

Columbia Road Flower Market

London's most colourful street market – and the capital's only dedicated flower market – Columbia Road grew from the seeds of a 19th-century food market surrounded by splendid Victorian shops. The area went into decline in the '70s and the historic street faced demolition, but a local campaign saved it and the market blossomed again in the '80s, boosted by the increasing popularity of TV gardening programmes.

On Sundays Columbia Road is transformed into an oasis of foliage and flowers – everything from bedding plants to 10-foot banana trees. Traders, many of whom are second or third generation and grow as well as sell their produce, offer a wide range of plants, bedding plants, shrubs, bulbs and freshly-cut flowers at competitive prices (which fall even lower near closing time).

The street offers much more than just a flower market and encompasses over 50 independent shops, making it one of East London's most interesting shopping streets. Outlets include tiny art galleries, cupcake vendors, perfumers, vintage clothing boutiques, homeware shops, English and Italian delis, garden accessory vendors, jewellery makers and antique dealers, plus more unusual wares such as hand-made soap, candlesticks and Buddhist artefacts. There's also a wealth of excellent pubs, cafés and restaurants. It's a great place to spend a relaxing Sunday.

Columbia Road Flower Market, Columbia Rd, E2 7RG (020-7613 0876; www.columbiaroad.info; Hoxton rail; Sun 8am-3pm).

Covent Garden Market

The first Covent Garden market dates back to 1654, although the current market buildings date from the 19th and early 20th centuries. These were originally the home of London's famous fruit & veg and flower market, which moved to Nine Elms in 1974 and is now known as New Covent Garden Market (www. newcoventgardenmarket.com). Since then the buildings have been occupied by a number of miscellaneous markets and have become a popular local and tourist attraction.

The colonnaded Piazza building houses the Apple Market – with stalls selling British-made souvenirs, unique fashion, jewellery, artworks, beauty products, collectibles and gifts, plus specialty shops, boutiques and cafés – while the East Colonnade offers similar wares, including handmade soap, jewellery, handbags, hand-knitted children's clothing, a magician's stall, sweets and homewares.

The South Piazza's Jubilee Hall (1904) is home to the Jubilee Market. Mondays are given over to antiques; from Tuesday to Friday there are stalls selling household goods, clothing, food and gifts; and on weekends the market is devoted to arts and crafts, with over 200 artisans selling everything from candles to jewellery, paintings to clocks and calligraphy. This London institution may appear too touristy and crowded to provide a traditional retail experience, but it's fun and you never know what you're going to find.

Covent Garden, WC2E 8BE (020-7836 9136/7379 4242; www.coventgardenlondonuk.com/markets and http://jubileemarket.co.uk; Covent Gdn tube; Jubilee Market, Mon 5am-5pm, Tue-Fri 10.30am-7pm, Sat-Sun 10am-6pm; Apple Market, Mon 9am-7pm, Tue-Sun 10.30am-7pm).

Farmers' & Food Markets

London pioneered the late 20th-century popularity of farmers' markets in the UK and they can now be found throughout the capital from Alexandra Palace to Wimbledon, providing a lifeline for small producers and vendors selling fresh, often organic and (most importantly) locally-produced food. There are also a number of small independent food markets throughout London (see below) in addition to farmers' markets and those featured elsewhere in this chapter.

There's a rule that everything on sale at farmers' markets should have been grown, reared, caught, brewed, pickled, baked, smoked or processed by the stallholder (with the exception of imported foods), or as London Farmers' Markets simply state, 'we grow it, we sell it'.

Farmers' Markets: A farmers' market is an event where food is sold directly to the public by farmers, growers and producers, with no middleman. Ranging in size from well-established food fairs to a small collection of stalls, they're united by the premium produce they sell: from locally-grown fruit and vegetables (often organic) to hand-made foods such as cakes, dairy produce, preserves and sauces.

Produce on sale usually includes fruit and vegetables; fish, meat and poultry; eggs, cheese and other dairy products; bread, juices, preserves, olives/olive oil, wine, cider

> To trade at one of the capital's farmers' markets, producers must be located within 100mi (160km) of the M25, although many are much closer.

and cakes; plus more unusual things such as edible flowers, raw honey and buffalo mozzarella. Because it's seasonal, produce varies throughout the year, but you'll often find unusual varieties that aren't available in supermarkets, such as Tatsoi salad greens, striped or golden beetroot, and heritage varieties of fruit and veg.

As well as being a source of quality food, farmers' markets are good for the environment: everything is 'locally' produced, thus reducing food miles. Some farms are organic, while others use minimal amounts of chemicals.

There are over 30 farmers' markets across London, most held weekly on Saturdays or Sundays, although some are held on weekdays and a few only once a month.

Many of the best are certified by FARMA, the National Farmers' Retail & Markets Association (www.farma.org.uk/certification-farmers-market), which independently assesses and certifies farmers' markets around the country to ensure that they're the 'real deal'.

There are two main organisations for farmers' markets in London: London Farmers' Markets, with some 20 markets, and City & Country Farmers' Markets, with around ten. Their aims are to increase farm incomes; promote local and seasonal foods; encourage sustainable agriculture, traditional animal breeds and heritage fruit and vegetable varieties; and further understanding between rural and urban communities. The websites (see below) have a list of markets, while the LFM website also provides a roll call of regular stallholders, maps and other information.

Other Food Markets: In addition to farmer's markets marketed by the organisations noted above, there are also

a number of independent food markets in London specialising in artisan, sustainable, local, organic and wholesome food that's usually sold directly by the producers or importers. These include Brockley Market (www.brockleymarket.com; Sat 10am-2pm), Crystal Palace Food Market (www.crystalpalacefoodmarket.co.uk; Sat 10am-3pm), Hackney Heart (www.hackneyheart.com, Sat 10am-5pm), Lower Marsh Market (www.wearewaterloo.co.uk/market; Mon-Sat 10am-5pm) and Venn Street Market (www.vennstreetmarket.co.uk; Sat 10am-4pm).

London Farmers' Markets (www.lfm.org.uk) and City & Country Farmers' Markets (www.wareccfm.com).

Greenwich Market

Greenwich has had a market since the 14th century, although the present one dates from 1700 when a charter to run a Wednesday and Saturday market for 1,000 years was assigned by Lord Romney to the Commissioners of Greenwich Hospital. Set in a courtyard of elegant Georgian buildings, the market is actually made up of three markets: the Antiques and Crafts Market, the Village Market and the Central Market.

Regarded by many as London's best market, it has up to 40 stalls offering antiques and collectibles on Tue and Thu-Fri; and arts, crafts and design (including fashion and jewellery) on Wed and Fri-Sun. There's also delicious street food, which may range from Thai noodles and Chinese dim sum to Punjabi rogan josh, Israeli falafel and Japanese sushi to Spanish tapas.

The unique covered market has a vibrant atmosphere and a commitment to showcasing designer-creators offering original artwork and toys, fashion and jewellery, as well as vendors of delicious fresh and artisan food. Plus it's surrounded by shops, cafés and pubs which open daily (grab a cuppa at the George café or a pint in the Coach & Horses). Not surprisingly, the market is one of Greenwich's main attractions and a destination in its own right.

Greenwich Market, SE10 9HZ (020-8269 5096; www.greenwichmarketlondon.com; Cutty Sark DLR; Tue-Sun 10am-5.30pm, closed Mon).

Leadenhall Market

Dating back to the 1300s, the original Leadenhall Market was largely destroyed in the Great Fire of 1666 and was rebuilt as a covered structure, when it was divided into a Beef Market, Green Yard and Herb Market. It was demolished in 1881 and rebuilt by Sir Horace Jones (1819-1887), architect of Billingsgate and Smithfield

Markets. The ornate wrought iron and glass structure, in shades of green, maroon and cream, is Grade II* listed and a major tourist attraction.

It's also popular with film directors and has featured in a number of films, including Clint Eastwood's *Hereafter*, Terry Gilliam's *The Imaginarium of Dr Parnassus*, and *Harry Potter and the Philosopher's Stone*, where the market stood in for Diagon Alley.

Leadenhall Market sells some of the finest food in the City, including fresh meat, cheese and delicacies from around the world, and has a variety of other vendors

including a florist, a chocolate shop, a pen shop and fashion boutiques, plus a number of restaurants, pubs (try the Lamb Tavern) and wine bars. It isn't just a commercial hub but also a lovely place to stroll around; a varied programme of events means the area is always bustling.

Leadenhall Market, Gracechurch St, EC3V 1LR (020-7332 1523; www.cityoflondon.gov.uk/things-to-do/leadenhall-market; Bank tube; Mon-Fri 10am-6pm, closed Sat-Sun).

Leather Lane Market

One of London's lesser-known but most interesting markets, Leather Lane Market in the City can trace its history back

some 400 years. Down to earth, slightly scruffy and incredibly diverse, it's what all traditional London street markets used to look like. Acting as a link between the busy main streets of Clerkenwell Road and High Holborn, the Lane (together with the jewellery quarter of Hatton Garden which runs parallel) is part of a vibrant historic neighbourhood laid out in the medieval period.

The lunch-time market sells a bit of everything, from fruit and vegetables to DVDs and mobile phones, clothing and footwear to flowers and travel accessories, all at bargain prices. You never know what you might find at the Lane. The market also offers a wealth of street food from a host of food stalls and cafés, from falafel

wraps and burritos to hog roasts and jacket potatoes, Italian delis to curry kiosks – and not a McDonalds or Starbucks in sight (but there is Prufrock Coffee!).

Leather Lane Market is a breath of fresh air: exuberant, colourful, a little bit bolshie, with characterful, cheerful traders, it's a treasure and a great place to browse.

Leather Lane Market, Leather Ln, EC1N 7RJ (www.leatherlanestars.wordpress.com/the-market; Chancery Ln or Farringdon tube; Mon-Fri 10am-2pm, closed Sat-Sun).

Maltby Street/ Ropewalk Market

Maltby Street in Bermondsey is one of London's newest foodie destinations, where the indie trader spirit thrives. The area between Maltby Street, Millstream Road and the nearby Ropewalk hosts a lively, informal weekend street market, with a combination of railway arch shops, open

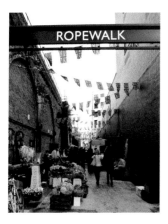

stalls, pop-up bars and eateries. It's a more laid back and relaxed affair than nearby Borough Market (see page 201) and has a burgeoning reputation among chefs and foodies.

The market (known variously as Maltby Street Market or Ropewalk Market) grew from an informal Saturday community after Monmouth Coffee roastery decided to open its doors for a few hours each week. They were swiftly followed by Neal's Yard Dairy, the Kappacasein Dairy and the Ham & Cheese Co. A few years on some of the old

traders have moved down the road to the Spa Terminus (see www. spa-terminus.co.uk) and newcomers have moved in.

At weekends, trestle tables heave with everything from cupcakes and brownies to seafood and charcuterie, gourmet gelato to oven-fresh bread and a

profusion of fruit and vegetables. You can also enjoy a local gin-based cocktail, artisan beers from the Kernel Brewery, wine and sherry from José Pizarro's tapas bar, and – of course – delicious Monmouth coffee.

Maltby Street Market, Ropewalk, Maltby St, SE1 3PA (www.maltby.st; Bermondsey tube; Sat 9am-4pm, Sun 11am-4pm).

Partridges Food Market

West London's most popular food market, Partridges (named after the nearby upmarket food emporium – see page 144) began life in 2005 and has grown rapidly in popularity ever since, attracting an average of 70 traders every Saturday (there's a waiting list for stalls). Held in Duke of York Square (close to Sloane Square tube station), the market offers a wide range of produce including free-range meats; patisserie, pastries and cakes; organic juices and produce; artisan bread and cheese; fish and seafood; homemade pies; specialist coffees and teas; and a wide range of international specialities and street food. See the website for a list of traders.

Partridges Food Market, Duke of York Sq, SW3 4LY (020-7730 0651; www.partridges.co.uk/ foodmarket; Sloane Sq tube; Sat 10am-4pm).

Petticoat Lane Market

A famous Sunday market operating since the 1750s, Petticoat Lane was named after the petticoats and lace sold there by the Huguenots who came to London from France in the 17th century (the street was renamed Middlesex Street in the 19th century by prudish Victorians who wanted to avoid references to women's underwear, but the name had stuck). Every Sunday it hosts more than 1,000 stalls spread over two streets, specialising in new goods ranging from clothing (particularly leather) and shoes to kitchenalia and household goods. It's one of London's oldest street markets and for bargain hunting – haggling is essential – it's the original and the best.

Petticoat Lane Market, Middlesex St, E1 7JF (Aldgate/Aldgate E/Liverpool St tube; Sun 9am-2pm).

Portobello Market

London's largest and most popular market, Portobello has been operating for over 150 years, and although most famous for its Saturday antiques market (see page 30), there's much more to it. It's several markets rolled into one and includes Portobello Green Market and Golborne Road Market, in addition to the famous antiques bazaar. On Fridays and Saturdays stalls stretch for a mile along Portobello Road and round the corner into Golborne Road.

Portobello Green is London's principal vintage, retro and boutique fashion market with up to 800 stalls. The market operates from Friday to Sunday under the Westway flyover on Portobello Road, offering mainly retro and vintage fashion and accessories (plus collectibles and bric-a-brac) on Fridays; designer clothes, accessories and jewellery on Saturdays; and bric-a-brac, vintage clothes, books, CDs and records, etc. on Sundays.

From Monday to Wednesday, Golborne Road hosts one of London's best fruit and veg markets, and Londoners flock from miles around to buy produce there (there are stalls selling bric-a-brac, household goods, clothing, furniture, etc. as well). There's a wide variety of specialist food stalls on most days, but Fridays and Saturdays are the best days for foodies and street-food addicts.

Portobello Market, Elgin Cres to Talbot Rd, W11 (www.portobelloroad.co.uk, www.portobellomarket.org, http://portobellofashionmarket.com and http://shopportobello.co.uk; Notting Hill Gate/Ladbroke Grove tube; Mon-Wed 9am-6pm, Thu 9am-1pm, Fri-Sat 9am-7pm, closed Sun).

St Katharine Docks World Food Market

One of the city's most popular street food venues, the World Food Market is held on Fridays in picturesque St Katharine Docks in East London. Situated in a lovely

location on Marble Quay overlooking the marina (outside the Dickens Inn), the lunch-time market attracts some 25 food stalls. Traders are noted for their healthy menus and for using ingredients that are, whenever possible, ethically and local sourced. There's a global menu stretching from South America to the Far East, including Argentinian prime steak sandwiches, Burmese noodles, Jamaican curried goat, Spanish paella, Turkish mezze, and even British stew and dumplings.

World Food Market, St Katharine Docks, Marble Quay, E1W 1UH (www.skdocks.co.uk/what's-on/friday-food-market; Tower Hill tube; Fri 11am-3pm).

Shepherd's Bush Market

Dating back to the early part of the 20th century, Shepherd's Bush Market is a vibrant exotic multicultural market (a world apart from the nearby Westfield shopping centre), serving the local Irish and Afro-Caribbean communities. A real local market, it's great for fresh foods, particularly fruit and veg (including unusual varieties like breadfruit, cassava and yams), fish, meat, spices and sauces; plus household goods, CDs, clothes and accessories, jewellery, fabrics and furnishings.

The market also hosts special themed events such as the Little Feast in summer 2016, a street-food festival in an English walled garden (www.wefeast.co.uk).

Shepherds Bush Market, railway viaduct between Uxbridge and Goldhawk Rds, W12 8LH (020-8749 3042; www.shepherdsbushmarket.co.uk and http://myshepherdsbushmarket.com; Shepherd's Bush Mkt tube; Mon-Sat 9am-6pm, closed Sun).

Smithfield Market

This monument to the meat trade dates back over 800 years and is the last surviving historical wholesale market in central London. It's housed in an imposing Victorian edifice (Grade II* listed) and is worth visiting for its architecture as much as its meat. The Italian-inspired market building was designed by Sir Horace Jones – the man who built Tower Bridge – and opened in 1868. The main wings (the East and West Market) are separated by the Grand Avenue, a wide roadway roofed by an elliptical arch: the whole is a vast cathedral-like structure of ornamental cast iron, stone, Welsh slate and glass.

Although Smithfield is primarily a wholesale market, anyone can buy meat there, although to get the best choice you need to arrive before 7am. The market's website advises that before buying anything you should have a good look around and ask questions – prices aren't normally displayed – and, if you're going to be buying regularly, get to know the traders too. But it's a fascinating place to visit even if you don't plan on shopping.

After your visit treat you can treat yourself to a hearty breakfast at one of the local pubs, which open early to serve the market traders.

Smithfield Market, EC1A 9PS (020-7248 3151; www.smithfieldmarket.com; Barbican tube; Mon-Fri 2am until mid-morning).

Spitalfields Traders Market

Once a Sunday-only mainstay, Spitalfields is now a seven-days-a-week destination. Resplendent under a glass canopy designed by Fosters & Partners, Spitalfields Traders Market – with

over 100 stalls on its busiest days – offers cutting-edge contemporary and vintage fashion, bespoke children's toys, jewellery and accessories, home interiors, original artworks and tasty food. There's also a Saturday Style Market (11am-5pm) and an Arts Market (on Market Street) on selected Sundays (see website) – and the antique hunters' much-loved Old Spitalfields Market (see page 27) is right next door. When you've had your fill of the market, there's a host of independent boutiques, food shops, cafés and restaurants nearby.

Spitalfields Traders Market, Brushfield St, E1 6AA (020-7377 1496; www.spitalfields.co.uk/ spitalfields-traders-market; Liverpool St tube/rail; Mon-Sat 10am-5pm, Sun 9am-5pm).

Walthamstow Market

Dating back to 1885, Walthamstow market is the longest outdoor street market in Europe, extending to over half a mile along Walthamstow High Street between Cleveland Park Avenue and Pretoria Avenue. Held Tuesday to Saturday, the market consists of up to 500 stalls selling an array of food (particularly Asian and Caribbean produce), flowers, fabrics, bric-a-brac, clothes, household goods and more, complemented by a wide variety of cafés, restaurants and pubs selling everything from Asian cuisine to traditional Cockney fare such as pie and mash and jellied eels. There's also a Sunday farmers' market (10am-2pm) on the Town Square (www.lfm. org.uk/markets/walthamstow).

Walthamstow Market, Walthamstow High St, E17 7JY (https://en.wikipedia.org/wiki/walthamstow_ market; Walthamstow Central tube/rail or Queen's Rd rail; Tue-Fri 8am-5pm, Sat 8am-5.30pm, closed Sun-Mon).

Whitechapel Market

Situated between Vallance Road and Cambridge Heath Road, Whitechapel Market is a long-established local market and social hub that unites the area's different cultures. A visit to this bustling market with its exotic sights, smells and sounds is like being deposited in Dhaka or Delhi – an exotic assault on the senses. Stalls offer just about every Asian ingredient, herb or spice you'll ever want, from cumin to coriander, cardamom to cloves,  plus a wide range of exotic fruit and vegetables and other Asian foods. You can also buy cut-price toiletries, cheap fashion, haberdashery, ethnic jewellery, flowers, fabrics and household goods. Great value and good fun!

Whitechapel Market, Whitechapel Rd, E1 1DT (Whitechapel/Aldgate E tube; Mon-Sat 9am-6pm, closed Sun).

Whitecross Street Market

One of London's oldest markets, Whitecross Street Market began trading in the 17th century. Today it's one of the capital's coolest shopping destinations, home to a weekday market selling everything from electrical and household items to clothing and handcrafted jewellery. However, it's the superb lunchtime street food that draws the crowds. You can choose from a wide range of cuisines and dishes including fresh salads, homemade pork pies, pie and mash, hog roast or salt beef sandwiches, wild game and more, plus mouth-watering cakes, pastries and cookies – and pretty much everything costs around £5 or less. The widest choice is from 12am-2pm and the best days are Thursdays and Fridays.

Whitecross Street Market, Whitecross St, EC1V 9AB (Barbican tube; Mon-Fri 10am-5pm, closed Sat-Sun).

V&A Museum Shop

10.
Miscellaneous

This chapter contains a selection of London's more unusual shops – the ones that aren't easily categorised – and includes both traditional traders, niche businesses and even a couple of, ahem, sex shops.

If you're looking for something unique or unusual, then London is a great place to shop, with its abundance of specialist, quirky and funky shops. From Alice Through the Looking Glass (a paean to all things Lewis Carroll) to James Smith's exquisite umbrellas, from Mungo & Maud's posh pet gear to the virtually indefinable Hoxton Street Monster Supplies, you'll find a little bit of everything in London's specialist shops: imaginative gifts, bizarre souvenirs and a slice of history, with something to appeal to everyone.

Whether it's a new shotgun or a venerable wig, a personal rubber stamp or some kinky rubber gear, a Batman costume or a jar of brain jam, a ship's bell or a bullet-proof vest, a box of Montecristos or a taxidermist for your dear departed cat − or perhaps you need to raise some serious cash to pay for all your purchases – the outlets in this chapter can fill your every need, however particular or peculiar. Even if you aren't planning on buying, they're wonderful places to browse…

Alice Through the Looking Glass

Opened in 2012, this charming boutique in Covent Garden specialises in Alice iconography including first-edition books, rare illustrated imprints and other related unique objects of desire. The shop is a treasure trove of Wonderland-inspired knick-knacks and curios, from framed illustrations to Victorian top hats, chess pieces to chocolates. The company also commissions new collections based on heritage pieces, handmade by British artists.

Co-founder Jake Fior (secondhand book dealer and former producer for Pete Doherty) was inspired to launch Alice after discovering Sir John Tenniel's original hand-painted 'Through the Looking Glass' chessboard. A fascinating piece of Alice iconography, the chessboard contains 16 illustrations around its border which are the earliest known examples of Tenniel's intended colouring for his Alice illustrations (featured in the original edition of the book). The original chessboard is displayed in the

shop and is worth an estimated £350,000 – although you can buy a limited edition handmade copy with gold leaf gilding (a snip at £3,500).

Not so curiously, Alice Through the Looking Glass has a resident giant white rabbit, Harley, who lives in a little burrow beneath the shop frontage and can often be seen in the window.

Alice Through the Looking Glass, 14 Cecil Ct, WC2N 4HE (020-7836 8854; http://alicelooking. co.uk; Leicester Sq tube; Mon-Fri 11am-6pm, Sat noon-5pm, closed Sun).

Altea Gallery

Founded by Massimo De Martini in 1992, the Altea Gallery in Mayfair is an antique map dealer offering a huge selection of original rare and vintage maps, charts, antique prints, atlases, reference books and old globes. The gallery's earliest maps date back to 1477 and the range includes everything from miniature maps to large-scale wall maps, town plans to sea charts, battle plans to celestial maps. All maps are sold with a certificate of authenticity and free advice is provided on collecting and investing in antique maps.

There's also a permanent exhibition of old maps of London, City of London plans and panoramas.

Altea Gallery, 35 St George St, W1S 2FN (020-7491 0010; http://alteagallery.com; Oxford Circus tube; Mon-Fri 10am-6pm, Sat 10am-4pm, closed Sun).

Angels Fancy Dress

From modest beginnings in 1813, when young tailor Daniel Angel arrived from Frankfurt and sold secondhand clothes from a barrow in Seven Dials, this family-run business has grown into one of the world's largest costumiers. The Shaftesbury Avenue premises house six floors of fancy dress costumes for sale or public hire, and there's a warehouse in Hendon packed with film and TV stock.

Angels can supply single or multiple costumes for parties and special occasions, along with a vast range of accessories such as wigs and masks. They even have costumes for your dog!

Angels Fancy Dress, 119 Shaftesbury Ave, WC2H 8AE (020-7836 5678; www.fancydress.com; Leicester Sq tube; Mon-Tue, Thu-Fri 9.30am-5.30pm, Wed 10.30am-7pm, closed Sat-Sun).

Arthur Beale

A rather surprising shop to find in the heart of the capital, Arthur Beale is a reminder that London was (indeed still is) an important port. This old-fashioned yacht chandler has changed little in the last 120 years. Though established here in the late 1800s, the business was begun by rope-maker John Buckingham alongside the Fleet River in the 16th century. It was saved from closure in 2014 when it was purchased by veteran sailor and theatrical chandler Alasdair Flint and his business partner Gerry Jeatt.

Arthur Beale trades in nautical equipment, everything from reels of rope (they produce rope and rigging to order) and ship's bells to nautical books and lifejackets.

Arthur Beale, 194 Shaftesbury Ave, WC2H 8JP (020-7836 9034; http://arthurbeale.co.uk; Tottenham Court Rd tube; Mon-Wed 9am-6pm, Thu-Fri 9am-8pm, Sat 10am-8pm, Sun 11am-5pm).

G Baldwin & Co

A family business dating back to 1844 – George Baldwin opened his first shop at 77 Walworth Road – this 'purveyor of natural products' is now owned by the Dagnell family, and is London's oldest herbalist and a south London institution.

G Baldwin captures the nostalgic atmosphere of the original shop, with wooden floors, old-fashioned counters, and shelves stacked with medicinal herbs, essential oils and natural remedies. But don't let appearances deceive you, the owners have moved with the times and offer an extensive range of quality products – from aromatherapy oils to health foods – and all at an affordable price.

G Baldwin & Co, 171-173 Walworth Rd, SE17 1RW (020-7703 5550; www.baldwins.co.uk; Elephant & Castle tube; Mon-Wed, Fri-Sat 9am-6pm, Thu 9am-7pm, closed Sun).

Berwick Street Cloth Shop

One of London's best fabric retailers, the Berwick Street Cloth Shop is part of a group of three shops and stockrooms in the heart of Soho, offering an extensive and diverse range of materials. The shop has been supplying the theatrical, film and television industries in the UK and worldwide for 20 years, and is a magnet for the fashion world. Its client list includes everyone from college students to world-famous designers, and its fabrics have graced catwalks, red carpets and high streets across the globe.

From silks to brocades, the choice of fabrics on sale is vast and tempting. Try to catch one of its seasonal remnant sales (see website for details).

Berwick Street Cloth Shop, 14 Berwick St, W1F 0PP (020-7287 2881; www. theberwickstreetclothshop.com; Oxford/ Piccadilly Circus tube; Mon-Fri 9am-6pm, Sat 10am-6pm, closed Sun).

Blade Rubber Stamps

This unique shop in the heart of historic Bloomsbury (just around the corner from the British Museum) has the largest range of rubber stamps and accessories in London. Whether you're seeking a custom stamp for your business or a decorative stamp for home use, Blade has a vast range to choose from – plus inkpads and accessories – and can also provide expert advice on personalising your design. You can even design and order a rubber stamp online.

The shop has been going since 1993 and also stocks everything for scrapbook addicts, including glitter, stickers and buttons. It holds free demonstrations to help you improve your decorating skills.

Blade Rubber Stamps, 12 Bury Pl, WC1A 2JL (020-7831 4123; www.bladerubberstamps. co.uk; Holborn tube; Mon-Sat 10.30am-6pm, Sun 11.30am-4.30pm).

Coco de Mer

Founded in 2001 by Samantha 'Sam' Roddick – daughter of Body Shop founder Anita Roddick – Coco de Mer is one of London's most glamorous erotic emporiums (aka sex shops). The name comes from an exotic plant whose seed resembles the female form. The business was purchased in 2011 by Lovehoney and now markets itself as an upmarket erotic boutique selling sexy lingerie, latex clothing, sex toys, whips and books.

Coco de Mer runs 'salons', described as 'evenings of education for the boudoir and beyond', where you can learn new skills, tricks and techniques such as spanking and rope bondage. An unusual first date?

Coco de Mer, 23 Monmouth St, WC2H 9DD (020-7836 8882; www.coco-de-mer.com; Covent Gdn tube; Mon-Sat 11am-7pm, Sun noon-6pm).

Condor Cycles

Condor Cycles is the store of choice for roadies, racers and serious commuters in search of top-notch kit. A family-run business since 1948, it manufactures and sells frames, components, accessories and clothing for cycling enthusiasts.

Condor's range of beautiful road bikes is legendary and is the brand of choice for such cycling greats as Sir Bradley Wiggins. They're built to order on a bespoke basis; first choose your frame, then get it made to measure for your size and finally select your desired components and clothing. Condor Cycles also offers a wide range of products from leading brands, as well as servicing facilities.

Condor Cycles, 49-53 Gray's Inn Rd, WC1X 8PP (020-7269 6820; www.condorcycles.com; Chancery La tube; Mon-Tue, Thu-Fri 8am-6pm, Wed 8am-7.30pm, Sat 10am-5pm, closed Sun).

Cornelissen & Son

A world-famous supplier of art materials, Cornelissen & Son in Bloomsbury has provided canvases and stretchers for works by many famous artists including Rex Whistler, W. R. Sickert and Aubrey Beardsley. Founded in 1855 by Louis Cornelissen (a Belgian lithographer), the family connection ended in 1977 on the death of Len Cornelissen and the shop was reopened in 1979 by Nicholas Walt, the current owner.

Cornelissen has been a draw for art lovers for over 150 years and is worth a visit just soak up the evocative Victorian atmosphere. From the iconic green-painted frontage to the charming old-fashioned interior, little has changed since the 19th century, with soaring floor-to-ceiling shelves lined with scores of glass jars full of pigments and pastels. A favourite in art circles, it stocks a vast selection of paints – oils, acrylics, gouache,

watercolours, pastels, etc. – an extensive array of brushes, drawing and calligraphy supplies, gold leaf and other decorative effects, print materials, paper, canvas and a selection of books.

Despite its times-gone-by aura, Cornelissen is no museum piece; it remains a thriving business, bustling with art students, calligraphers and professional artists.

Cornelissen & Son, 105 Great Russell St, WC1B 3RY (020-7636 1045; www.cornelissen.com; Tottenham Court Rd tube; Mon-Sat 9.30am-6pm, closed Sun).

Davenports Magic

Established in 1898, Davenports is the oldest continuously-owned magic shop in the world and a one-stop shop for budding Harry Potters. The staff are all professional magicians, chosen for their in-depth knowledge of magic, who are more than happy to show you a trick or two as you wander around wide-eyed.

The store caters for all levels of illusionist, from complete beginners to seasoned professionals, and sells wands, magic tricks, magician's kits, books, tutorials,

and a wealth of accessories. Equipment for beginners includes card decks and coin tricks, while for more experienced magicians there's everything from top hats (minus the rabbit) to crafty tables for sawing the mother-in-law in half. There's also a wide selection of posters, collectibles, instructional DVDs and books (including an interesting secondhand section).

If you're keen to learn the tricks of the trade you can enrol in one of Davenports'

magic courses (see website for details). Available for children and adults, they aim to provide a good working knowledge of the fundamentals of magic.

Davenports Magic, 7 Charing Cross Underground Arcade, The Strand, WC2N 4HZ (020-7836 0408; www.davenportsmagic.co.uk; Charing Cross tube; Mon-Fri 9.30am-5.30pm, Sat 10.30am-4.30pm, closed Sun).

Ede & Ravenscroft

Thought to be the oldest firm of tailors in the world, Ede & Ravenscroft began trading in 1689 in Aldwych, then the centre of the tailoring trade. It was run by a respected tailoring family, the Shudalls, who were soon catering to royalty, church and state, academia and the legal profession.

For over 325 years the company has provided ceremonial robes for all occasions – including 12 coronations – dressed the judiciary (plus handmade wigs) and catered for graduation ceremonies throughout the world. Today, in addition to its robe and wig-making business, Ede & Ravenscroft provides bespoke tailoring, and a ready-to-wear collection that includes suits, shirts and accessories.

Ede & Ravenscroft, 93 Chancery Ln, WC2A 1DU (020-7405 3906; www.edeandravenscroft.com; Chancery Ln tube; Mon-Fri 8.45am-6pm, Sat 10am-3pm, closed Sun).

Forbidden Planet

Named after the 1956 feature film, Forbidden Planet is the world's largest and best-known science fiction, fantasy and cult entertainment retailer, and the largest UK stockist of comics and graphic novels. It began in 1978 as a small store in Denmark Street, Soho, and has traded from its London megastore since 2003.

The store specialises in selling action figures, books, comics (including DC, Marvel and manga), DVDs, video games, graphic novels, clothing and toys, and offers the best merchandise from the cream of cult movies and television, including *The Avengers*, *Batman*, *Breaking Bad*, *Doctor Who*, *Game Of Thrones*, *Star Trek*, *Star Wars*, *Transformers* and many more.

Forbidden Planet, 179 Shaftesbury Ave, WC2H 8JR (020-7420 3666; https://forbiddenplanet.com; Tottenham Court Rd tube; Mon-Tue 10am-7pm, Wed, Fri-Sat 10am-7.30pm, Thu 10am-8pm, Sun noon-6pm).

Hamleys

The oldest, largest and most famous toy shop in the world, Hamleys was founded in 1760 by William Hamley, moving to its flagship store on Regent Street in 1881. Today, the store covers seven floors, each devoted to a different category of toys, which include pre-school, soft toys, arts & crafts, dolls, build it, action toys, games, outdoor and vehicles.

Covering some 5,000m² and crammed with over 50,000 toys, Hamleys is one of the city's top tourist attractions, welcoming over 5 million visitors annually. It holds regular school-holiday events for children (see the website for details) and also hosts themed birthday parties.

Hamleys, 188-196 Regent St, W1B 5BT (0371-704 1977; www.hamleys.com; Oxford Circus tube; Mon-Fri 10am-9pm, Sat 9.30am-9pm, Sun noon-6pm).

D R Harris

Founded in 1790 in St James's by surgeon Henry Harris and chemist Daniel Rotely, D R Harris's apothecary established its reputation providing lavender water, classic cologne and English flower perfumes to this fashionable quarter of London (it holds two royal warrants for The Queen and The Prince of Wales). Visiting the shop is like stepping back a century or two; its polished wooden cabinets are crammed with bottles and jars containing old-fashioned shaving brushes and manicure kits.

Today, it's both a fully-functioning pharmacy and a perfumery, producing an extensive range of products including shaving creams and soaps, aftershave, cologne, skincare products and much more.

D R Harris, 29 St James's St, SW1A 1HB (020-7930 3915; www.drharris.co.uk; Green Pk tube; Mon-Fri 8.30am-6pm, Sat 9.30am-5pm, closed Sun).

Holland & Holland

Established by Harris Holland in 1835, Holland & Holland is a prestigious manufacturer and retailer of handmade sporting shotguns and rifles. Its flagship store in Mayfair is home to a magnificent gun room where visitors can browse the collection of new and pre-owned shotguns and rifles, along with a comprehensive range of cartridges and other ammunition. The gun room also provides services for the discerning shooter, including gun storage, maintenance, repairs and renovation.

The store also offers a huge selection of the best shooting accessories – from hip flasks to cartridge belts – plus clothing, including shooting attire and safari gear, and a vast choice of gifts.

Holland & Holland, 33 Bruton St, W1J 6HH (020-7499 4411; https://hollandandholland.com; Bond St tube; Mon-Fri 9am-6pm, Sat 10am-5pm, closed Sun).

Hoxton Street Monster Supplies

London's 'oldest supplier of goods for the living, dead and undead', Hoxton Street Monster Supplies is one of London's wackiest shops. The intriguing store is part of the Ministry of Stories (http://ministryofstories.org), an East London initiative whereby professional writers mentor young people in the art of story writing, with profits going to the charity.

This is London's only purveyor of quality goods for monsters; whether you're a vampire, werewolf or some other non-human life form, the store has everything you could need. Its pharmacopoeia of delights includes tinned fear, a complete range of edible human preserves, and everyday household essentials such as brain jam, fang floss and edible earwax. Yum!

Hoxton Street Monster Supplies, 159 Hoxton St, N1 6PJ (020-7729 4159; www.monstersupplies. org; Hoxton rail; Tue-Fri 1-5pm, Sat 11am-5pm, closed Sun-Mon).

James J. Fox

The world's oldest cigar merchants, James J. Fox traces its story back to 1787 when Robert Lewis began trading in fine tobacco in St James's Street. James

J. Fox – formed in Dublin in 1881 and trading in London since 1947 – acquired the business of Robert Lewis in 1992, thus uniting two of the most respected names in the cigar world. Both companies now trade as JJ Fox (St James's) Ltd. which operates the cigar departments at both Harrods and Selfridges. The company specialises in premium and Cuban cigars – including Churchill's favourite Montecristos – cigar smokers' accessories such as humidors, pipes and pipe tobacco, smoking paraphernalia and a limited range of superior cigarettes.

Over the companies' combined more than 225 years in business, customers have included discriminating smokers from all walks of life – from commoners to kings – including Sir Winston Churchill, Oscar Wilde, British and foreign royalty, the officers' mess of famous British regiments, and the

leading lights of stage, film, sport, TV, radio, music and literature.

Today, the shop is one of very few retail outlets in London exempt from the smoking ban, where it's possible to enjoy your purchase to your heart's content wreathed in sumptuous blue smoke. There's also a bijoux cigar museum.

James J. Fox, 19 St James's St, SW1A 1ES (020-7930 3787; www.jjfox.co.uk; Green Pk tube; Mon-Wed, Fri 9.30am-8pm, Thu 9.30am-8.45pm, Sat 9.30am-5pm, closed Sun).

James Smith & Sons

The home of the London umbrella and famous around the world, James Smith & Sons is a family-run business that's been making umbrellas, sticks and canes since 1830. The historic shop on New Oxford Street dates back to 1867 and still has its original brass and mahogany shop front and hand-crafted interior fittings – made by the master craftsman employed by the business

– a nostalgic reminder of Victorian times. The workshops are located in the basement, where umbrellas and walking sticks are still made today (although due to high demand, many are now made by other small family firms).

James Smith has always thrived, thanks to London's unpredictable weather, its outstanding reputation and the repair service they

offer. The design and materials of the gentleman's traditional umbrella have changed little over the years, apart from the fact that most of the covers are now made from nylon.

James Smith's devotion to quality is admirable, though prices are correspondingly high, so you may need to save for a rainy day to buy one!

James Smith & Sons, 53 New Oxford St, WC1A 1BL (020-7836 4731; www.james-smith.co.uk; Tottenham Court Rd tube; Mon-Tue, Thu-Fri 10am-5.45pm, Wed 10.30am-5.45pm, Sat 10am-5.15pm, closed Sun).

Lillywhites

The Lillywhite family hold a firm place in cricketing folklore – William Lillywhite is credited with the introduction of round-arm bowling – and it's said that when the first Lillywhites store opened in Haymarket in 1863 it sold nothing but cricket bats and cigars! However, it soon added other sports equipment and quickly gained a reputation for its quality products. In 1866,

its No 5 football was the first ball ever specified for a Football Association (soccer) match, and in the same year, the Ivy League selected its 'No J' American football as the standard college football.

In 1925 Lillywhites moved to its current home, an elegant Victorian building – with an amazing ornate ceiling and spectacular dome – on Regent Street. Its design and location made it one of London's most iconic stores.

Lillywhites Piccadilly is the world's largest sports store with 34 specialist sport departments over six floors, covering everything from aerobics to yoga. The firm was bought in 2002 by Sports Direct International plc, Britain's biggest retailer of sports clothing and accessories – best known for its low prices – but Lillywhites remains the go-to destination for quality sports equipment and clothing, and attracts customers from far and wide.

Lillywhites, 24-36 Regent St, SW1Y 4QF (0344-332 5602; www.lillywhites.com; Piccadilly Circus tube; Mon-Sat 9.30am-10pm, Sun 11.45am-6pm).

London Taxidermy

This fascinating business was founded by Alexis Turner, author of *Taxidermy* (2013, Thames & Hudson) and an expert in the subject, though not a taxidermist himself. Alexis has been buying, selling and hiring out natural history artefacts for over 20 years, and has a wide range of specimens, including stuffed birds and animals, big

game heads, trophy horns, antlers, skulls, skeletons, pickled specimens, curiosities, butterflies and beetles.

If you want to get some antlers mounted, buy a stuffed owl and a vintage glass dome to go over it, or hire a stuffed giraffe for a party, Alexis is your man. All specimens hired and sold at London Taxidermy have been obtained legally – and ethically.

London Taxidermy, Unit 38, Wimbledon Stadium Business Centre, Riverside Rd, SW17 0BA (020-8947 4873; www.londontaxidermy.com; Earlsfield rail; Mon-Sat by appointment).

Mungo & Maud

The boutique of choice for posh pooches and cool cats, Mungo & Maud was the brainchild of Michael and Nicola Sacher, who opened their store in Belgravia in 2005. The company offers a range of stylish, design-led accessories with a creative edge, made from natural materials such as wool, leather and linen.

The collection is minimalist yet tactile, and ranges from hand-stitched leather collars to wooden feeding bowls, cotton beds and organic treats to a wealth of amusing accessories for the most discerning cats and dogs – all made to Mungo & Maud's own recipe. There are some nifty ideas for humans too, including bags, books, gifts and walking accessories such as poop bag pouches.

Mungo & Maud, 79 Elizabeth St, SW1W 9PJ (020-7467 0823; www.mungoandmaud.com; Sloane Sq tube; Mon-Sat 10am-6pm, closed Sun).

Mysteries Shop

The world-famous Mysteries Shop in Covent Garden is the UK's premier new age and metaphysical resource centre, a world away from the tourist mayhem outside its door. It's the perfect place to get in touch with your spiritual side – a mecca of mysticism – and a one-stop shop for body, mind and soul enthusiasts. Mysteries has been raising spirits since 1982 and is a

cornucopia of all things spiritual and other-worldly, from glittering natural crystals to crystal balls of all sizes, candles to tarot cards, and Tibetan singing bowls to dream catchers, swinging lazily from the ceiling. There's also a wealth of occult and self-help books, divination implements, and spiritual CDs and DVDs.

Upstairs are meeting rooms where you can consult – either in person or via telephone – a wide range of clairvoyants, healers, psychics and mediums; have tarot card, aura and palm readings; and take part in various classes and courses including reiki, meditation, and sound and music healing. People from all walks of life visit Mysteries for insight and clarity about their lives and to discover what the future holds.

Mysteries Shop, 9 Monmouth St, WC2H 9DA (020-7240 3688; www.mysteries.co.uk; Covent Gdn tube; Mon-Sat 11am-6.30pm, Sun noon-6pm).

Phillo Flowers

Notting Hill 'floral design company' Phillo (meaning 'leaf' in Greek) specialises in innovative flower arrangements for weddings, private parties and corporate events such as product launches and film and television events. It was founded in 2003 by Cemal K Cemal whose floral arrangements – from bowls and hatboxes to bouquets – are renowned for their striking bespoke designs, using unusual flowers and foliage from around the globe.

Sharing the shop are Phillo's brightly-coloured parrots – blue-fronted amazons and blue and gold macaws – who take it in turn to visit the shop, happily chatting to customers and adding a certain sub-tropical glamour to proceedings.

Phillo Flowers, 59 Chepstow Rd, W2 5BP (020-7727 4555; www.philloflowers.com; Royal Oak tube; Mon-Sat 9.30am-7pm, Sun 10am-4pm).

Prestige Pawnbrokers

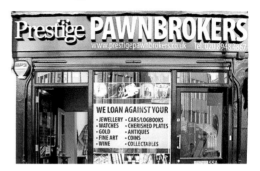

When you've squandered all your money on bling and need a bit of ready cash to tide you over, you can pop along to Prestige Pawnbrokers, made famous in the Channel 4 TV series *Posh Pawn*. Prestige will buy – or provide a loan against – jewellery, watches, gold, cars, art, designer handbags, antiques, fine wine, rare stamps, coins, rare books and just about anything else that's portable and has a (high) value.

Once you have accepted an offer they will instantly pay you in cash or via another pre-arranged method. The loan term is up to seven months and goods can be redeemed at any time on payment of the accrued interest.

Prestige Pawnbrokers, New House, 67-68 Hatton Gdn, EC1N 8JY (020-7405 6664; www. prestigepawnbrokers.co.uk; Farringdon tube/rail; Mon-Fri 9.30am-5pm, closed Sat-Sun).

Sh!

Set up in 1992 as an antidote to the sleazy, male-dominated sex industry of the time, Sh! is an award-winning erotic emporium run by women for women, providing a welcoming, honest and

informative environment where women can comfortably talk about sex and sex toys. The first women's sex shop in the UK, it has driven the sea change that has transformed views on female sexuality. Sh! offers a wealth of sensual and safe sex toys, including exclusive vibrators, lube, and its own artisan range of strap-on harnesses and dildos.

The shop also runs erotic classes and provides honest, upfront advice to help women explore their individual sexuality.

Sh!, 57 Hoxton Sq, N1 6PB (020-7613 5458; www. sh-womenstore.com; Old St tube/rail; daily noon-8pm).

Spymaster

London's most respected and best-equipped spy shop, Spymaster has been dealing in state-of-the-art surveillance, counter-surveillance, personal protection and security equipment since 1991. Not exactly a secret – although it does boast frosted glass – Spymaster is the perfect one-stop shop for covert missions, supplying everything from bullet-proof vests and chemical warfare suits to hidden cameras and bugging devices, and armoured and 'blast proof' vehicles. If there's a hi-tech gadget for it, you'll find it here.

Beneath the store are private rooms where you can discuss your needs and try out products. You can also hire bodyguards, private detectives and sniffer dogs.

Spymaster, 3 Portman Sq, W1H 6LB (020-7486 3885; www.spymaster.co.uk; Bond St/Marble Arch tube; Mon-Fri 9.30am-6.30pm, Sat 10am-5pm, closed Sun).

V&A Shop

The V&A Shop at the Victoria & Albert Museum in South Kensington – the world's greatest museum of art and design – is a destination in its own right and a treasure trove of over 6,000 products. The store stocks a broad range of beautiful original designs to suit all ages and pockets, as well as exclusive commissions, one-off vintage pieces and iconic products inspired by exhibits in the V&A's collections and temporary shows – in 2016 these included Botticelli Reimagined (cue Venus bath towels and pearl jewellery), The Fabric of India (glorious scarves and shawls) and Shoes: Pleasure and Pain (art school sticky plasters).There's a themed mini-shop for major exhibitions.

The wealth of all-year-round merchandise includes jewellery, furniture, books, textiles, toys, ceramics, fashion, design, glass and accessories, which are selected and commissioned from designers and artists throughout the world, such as Lulu Guinness, Helen David, Lizzie Montgomery and Walker + Walker.

The shop is a fascinating place to browse or find an unusual present, and there's also an excellent art bookshop. And when you've had your fill of shopping you can take a break in one of the museum's excellent cafés.

V & A Shop, Victoria & Albert Museum, Cromwell Rd, SW7 2RL (020-7942 2687; www.vandashop. com; S Kensington tube; daily 10am-5.30pm, Fri until 10pm).

INDEX OF ENTRIES BY AREA

City of London

East

Southeast

London Sketchbook

£10.95

ISBN: 978-1-907339-37-0
Jim Watson

A celebration of one of the world's great cities, London Sketchbook is packed with over 200 evocative watercolour illustrations of the author's favourite landmarks and sights. The illustrations are accompanied by historical footnotes, maps, walks, quirky facts and a gazetteer.

Also in this series:

Cornwall Sketchbook (ISBN: 9781907339417, £10.95)
Cotswold Sketchbook (ISBN: 9781907339108, £9.95)
Devon Sketchbook (ISBN: 9781909282704, £10.95)
Lake District Sketchbook (ISBN: 9781907339097, £9.95)
Yorkshire Sketchbook (ISBN: 9781909282773, £10.95)

see www.survivalbooks.net

INDEX

London's Best-Kept Secrets

ISBN: 978-1-909282-74-2, 320 pages, £10.95

David Hampshire

London Best-Kept Secrets brings together our favourite places – the 'greatest hits' – from our London's Secrets series of books. We take you off the beaten tourist path to seek out the more unusual ('hidden') places that often fail to register on the radar of both visitors and residents alike. Nimbly sidestepping the chaos and queues of London's tourist-clogged attractions, we visit its quirkier, lesser-known, but no less fascinating, side. *London Best-Kept Secrets* takes in some of the city's loveliest hidden gardens and parks, absorbing and poignant museums, great art and architecture, beautiful ancient buildings, magnificent Victorian cemeteries, historic pubs, fascinating markets and much more.

London's Hidden Corners, Lanes & Squares

ISBN: 978-1-909282-69-8, 192 pages, £9.95

Graeme Chesters

The inspiration for this book was the advice of writer and lexicographer Dr Samuel Johnson (1709-1784), who was something of an expert on London, to his friend and biographer James Boswell on the occasion of his trip to London in the 18th century, to 'survey its innumerable little lane and courts'. In the 21st century these are less numerous than in Dr Johnson's time, so we've expanded his brief to include alleys, squares and yards, along with a number of mews, roads, streets and gardens.

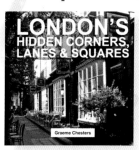

A Year in London: Two Things to Do Every Day of the Year

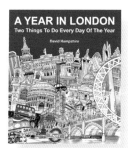

ISBN: 978-1-909282-68-1, 256 pages, £11.95

David Hampshire

London offers a wealth of things to do, from exuberant festivals and exciting sports events to a plethora of fascinating museums and stunning galleries, from luxury and oddball shops to first-class restaurants and historic pubs, beautiful parks and gardens to pulsating nightlife and clubs. Whatever your interests and tastes, you'll find an abundance of things to enjoy – with a copy of this book you'll never be at a loss for something to do in one of the world's greatest cities.

see www.londons-secrets.com

LONDON'S HIDDEN SECRETS

ISBN: 978-1-907339-40-0

£10.95, 320 pages

Graeme Chesters

A guide to London's hidden and lesser-known sights that aren't found in standard guidebooks. Step beyond the chaos, clichés and queues of London's tourist-clogged attractions to its quirkier side.

Discover its loveliest ancient buildings, secret gardens, strangest museums, most atmospheric pubs, cutting-edge art and design, and much more: some 140 destinations in all corners of the city.

LONDON'S HIDDEN SECRETS VOL 2

ISBN: 978-1-907339-79-0

£10.95, 320 pages

Graeme Chesters & David Hampshire

Hot on the heels of London's Hidden Secrets comes another volume of the city's largely undiscovered sights, many of which we were unable to include in the original book. In fact, the more research we did the more treasures we found, until eventually a second volume was inevitable.

Written by two experienced London writers, LHS 2 is for both those who already know the metropolis and newcomers wishing to learn more about its hidden and unusual charms.

LONDON'S SECRET PLACES

ISBN: 978-1-907339-92-9

£10.95, 320 pages

Graeme Chesters & David Hampshire

London is one of the world's leading tourist destinations with a wealth of world-class attractions. These are covered in numerous excellent tourist guides and online, and need no introduction here. Not so well known are London's numerous smaller attractions, most of which are neglected by the throngs who descend upon the tourist-clogged major sights. What London's Secret Places does is seek out the city's lesser-known, but no less worthy, 'hidden' attractions.

LONDON'S SECRET WALKS

ISBN: 978-1-907339-51-6

£11.95, 320 pages

Graeme Chesters

London is a great city for walking – whether for pleasure, exercise or simply to get from A to B. Despite the city's extensive public transport system, walking is often the quickest and most enjoyable way to get around – at least in the centre – and it's also free and healthy!

Many attractions are off the beaten track, away from the major thoroughfares and public transport hubs. This favours walking as the best way to explore them, as does the fact that London is a visually interesting city with a wealth of stimulating sights in every 'nook and cranny'.

see www.londons-secrets.com

LONDON'S SECRETS: BIZARRE & CURIOUS
ISBN: 978-1-909282-58-2
£11.95, 320 pages
Graeme Chesters

London is a city with 2,000 years of history, during which it has accumulated a wealth of odd and strange sights. This book seeks out the city's most bizarre and curious attractions and tells the often fascinating story behind them, from the Highgate vampire to the arrest of a dead man, a legal brothel and a former Texas embassy to Roman bikini bottoms and poetic manhole covers, from London's hanging gardens to a restaurant where you dine in the dark. *Bizarre & Curious* is sure to keep you amused and fascinated for hours.

LONDON'S SECRETS: MUSEUMS & GALLERIES
ISBN: 978-1-907339-96-7
£10.95, 320 pages
Robbi Atilgan & David Hampshire

London is a treasure trove for museum fans and art lovers and one of the world's great art and cultural centres. The art scene is a lot like the city itself – diverse, vast, vibrant and in a constant state of flux – a cornucopia of traditional and cutting-edge, majestic and mundane, world-class and run-of-the-mill, bizarre and brilliant.

So, whether you're an art lover, culture vulture, history buff or just looking for something to entertain the family during the school holidays, you're bound to find inspiration in London.

LONDON'S SECRETS: PARKS & GARDENS
ISBN: 978-1-907339-95-0
£10.95, 320 pages
Robbi Atilgan & David Hampshire

London is one the world's greenest capital cities, with a wealth of places where you can relax and recharge your batteries. Britain is renowned for its parks and gardens, and nowhere has such beautiful and varied green spaces as London: magnificent royal parks, historic garden cemeteries, majestic ancient forests and woodlands, breathtaking formal country parks, expansive commons, charming small gardens, beautiful garden squares and enchanting 'secret' gardens.

LONDON'S SECRETS: PUBS & BARS
ISBN: 978-1-907339-93-6
£10.95, 320 pages
Graeme Chesters

British pubs and bars are world famous for their bonhomie, great atmosphere, good food and fine ales. Nowhere is this more so than in London, which has a plethora of watering holes of all shapes and sizes: classic historic boozers and trendy style bars; traditional riverside inns and luxurious cocktail bars; enticing wine bars and brew pubs; mouth-watering gastro pubs and brasseries; welcoming gay bars and raucous music venues. This book highlights over 250 of the best.

see www.londons-secrets.com

London's Secrets: Peaceful Places

ISBN: 978-1-907339-45-5, 256 pages, hardback, £11.95
David Hampshire

London is one of the world's most exciting cities, but it's also one of the noisiest; a bustling, chaotic, frenetic, over-crowded, manic metropolis of over 8 million people, where it can be difficult to find somewhere to grab a little peace and quiet. Nevertheless, if you know where to look London has a wealth of peaceful places: places to relax, chill out, contemplate, meditate, sit, reflect, browse, read, chat, nap, walk, think, study or even work (if you must) – where the city's volume is muted or even switched off completely.

London for Foodies, Gourmets & Gluttons

ISBN: 978-1-909282-76-6, 288 pages, hardback, £11.95
David Hampshire & Graeme Chesters

Much more than simply a directory of cafés, markets, restaurants and food shops, *London for Foodies, Gourmets & Gluttons* features many of the city's best artisan producers and purveyors, plus a wealth of classes where you can learn how to prepare and cook food like the experts, appreciate fine wines and brew coffee like a barista. And when you're too tired to cook or just want to treat yourself, we'll show you great places where you can enjoy everything from tea and cake to a tasty street snack; a pie and a pint to a glass of wine and tapas; and a quick working lunch to a full-blown gastronomic extravaganza.

London's Cafés, Coffee Shops & Tearooms

ISBN: 978-1-909282-80-3, 192 pages, £9.95
David Hampshire

This book is a celebration of London's flourishing independent cafés, coffee shops and tearooms – plus places serving afternoon tea and breakfast/brunch – all of which have enjoyed a renaissance in the last decade and done much to strengthen the city's position as one of the world's leading foodie destinations. With a copy of *London's Cafés, Coffee Shops & Tearooms* you'll never be lost for somewhere to enjoy a great cup of coffee or tea and some delicious food.

see www.survivalbooks.net